Finding Success
After Failure:

How Psychosis Made Me
and Did Not Break Me

Erin Wall

Finding Success After Failure:
How Psychosis Made Me and Did Not Break Me

ISBN: 979-8-9871097-0-0

Printed in the United States of America

TABLE OF CONTENTS

INTRODUCTION

This book is an overview of my life since around 2015. How one relationship and one choice altered my life forever. And how strong a support system in family and close friends can turn someone's life around. I would not be where I am today without my Faith in God, my mother Allison, my father Kevin, my sister Greta, my brother-in-law Tyler, my Grandmother Diana and my best friend of sixteen years Vartouhy. I faced one of the scariest situations in my life that I will ever experience and if it was not for them I would not be here today.

I made a life-threatening choice one night in Chicago with my boyfriend which altered my life forever. I am forever grateful he was with me that night to help me through the whole ordeal.

Through my faith, family, therapy, prayer and sheer determination, I find success and recovery in the end.

Trigger warning, graphic content, this book mentions psychotic episodes and the use of illegal drugs, read with caution.

CHAPTER ONE

My Plan for Life

June 2017 to August 2017

What is your response when someone tells you a goal may not be attainable? Do you give heed to their worry, or continue to follow your own path? Sometimes following your own direction is beneficial, but, other times, it may lead you down a potentially detrimental path.

I always lived my life thinking I could accomplish anything I set my mind to. It was not until August of 2017 that life proved to be more challenging than I ever expected.

In May of 2017, my plans were to join the Navy as an Officer, uproot my life, and move across the country for Officer Candidate School (OCS). OCS is a life changing experience for all who attend, but my personal experience was life threatening as well as changing.

Getting accepted into OCS is no easy feat. Each year there are over 20,000 applicants for Navy OCS. Admission into OCS is extremely competitive. Out of all applicants, approximately ten percent are accepted.

When I applied for OCS, my job was going to be a Supply Officer. I had received my undergraduate degree in Business Administration and decided that would have been the best fit for my career.

Throughout college, I had never been the best at test taking. I had been getting by, but definitely needed more practice.

When applying for OCS, you have to take an exam to see where your knowledge base is and the results help determine acceptance or not.

The test is called Officer Aptitude Rating (OAR); it covers mechanical comprehension, math, reading, and consists of ninety questions.

I studied for months. Having always struggled with math, I got a tutor, and received the exact test score needed to pass. I was a little upset at that point because I knew I was not going to stand out with my test scores. I was feeling a bit discouraged but still decided to not give up hope and continue the application process.

With the help of my father, who had served for twenty-nine years in the Navy, and a few recommendations from Supply Officers, I was accepted. However, the recruiter taking care of my paperwork and that of many others mishandled the process. Although she was disciplined, my Military Entrance Processing Station (MEPS) appointment was delayed due to her irresponsibility.

I left for OCS in August of 2017, but if I had gone to MEPS earlier as I was supposed to, I may have left for OCS in June as originally planned.

Sometimes events are meant to be taken as a sign. Receiving such a minimally acceptable grade on the OAR and my original recruiter causing an unnecessary delay may have been signs but I was too hard-headed to see that as a possibility. I thought I could accomplish anything, and my objective was to make it into OCS and become a Naval Officer. I should have taken a step back and listened to the signs that maybe OCS was not for me.

Some events that took place at OCS were life changing, and I will forever live with the consequences and end result.

When I left for OCS, I had been living in San Diego, California. OCS is based in Rhode Island, so I had to fly east. I was leaving early in the morning and my father drove me to the airport before he went to work. I was extremely nervous and basically did not stop talking the entire car ride.

My father and mother were extremely worried, but I assured them I would be fine. I soon found out that I was wrong. Young twenty-three-year-olds always think they are right, and while they can be, it is important to listen to your parents sometimes.

When I arrived in Rhode Island, I booked a hotel room for the night and relaxed, preparing mentally for the next day. I received a good night's sleep, and when I woke up, I got dressed, ate some breakfast, and waited a few minutes for my ride onto base.

The military is an extremely tight-knit community, and my mother found a fellow military spouse, who drove me onto base and dropped me off at OCS. Upon arrival, I checked in and got some supplies including my sea bag. We were being given a tour and while the tour was going on, I had to lug all of my bags around. We were walking all over including up and down stairs and even outside. This resulted in me fainting from heat exhaustion before I was able to have my phone call, so I am sure I freaked my parents out when I told them on my first phone call that I had fainted within the first half hour. At that point, I am sure they were scared out of their minds for me. I still carried on and continued my journey at OCS, which may have been the wrong decision.

I come across people sometimes who are thinking of joining the Navy as an Officer. Although I was not there very long, I am still able to pass on wisdom to assist those in knowing more of what to expect. OCS was also my "what doesn't kill you makes you stronger" moment, and, for that, I am grateful. There are things I accomplished while at OCS that I am very proud of, and I will never regret attending. However, there are also dark moments that cast a shadow over those accomplishments, dimming their brightness in my mind.

I am not exactly sure what event at OCS triggered my psychotic break, but there were some issues I had been facing beforehand that helped the break occur. I had been dating a guy off and on for a few years before I left, sort of like a Ross and Rachel from the sitcom *Friends* situation. We had broken up again a few weeks prior to me leaving for OCS. Our relationship, at the time, was long distance because of his work, which had caused a lot of strain. We were fighting a lot, getting back together, breaking up, starting a "break", and also trying to figure out if we could make it work. We chose to get back together and make things work about a week or so before I left. I was over-joyed about having my boyfriend back, so we decided I would go visit him for a few days. What occurred on that trip altered my life forever.

CHAPTER TWO

Life's Plan for Me

Before I started training at OCS, I went to visit my boyfriend in Chicago. Shim and had been dating for almost three years at this point, but had broken up and gotten back together multiple times. Our relationship was always a little crazy. I met my boyfriend on Facebook, sort of. The day we met I had messaged him and had a plan to surprise a different guy I wanted to date. I wanted to take him and another friend up to a bar so they could all hang out, because they had not seen each other in years. I told him my plan and we decided to meet that day to talk over the plan a little bit more. We decided to meet at the Commissary on MCAS Miramar, a Marine Corps base in San Diego, CA. When we met, we talked over the plan a little bit more and had an understanding. We decided to pick up another friend before heading up to the bar.

Somehow I became the surprise because they called their friend, the one I was trying to surprise, and told him to meet them at the bar. Although I was trying to be nice and surprise this guy, he ended up ignoring me most of the night and dancing with other women. I decided to hang out with Shim most of the night. I concluded if the other guy was not interested, I should probably focus my efforts on Shim, who had seemed interested all day. That day at the commissary started mine and Shim's wild and passionate relationship.

Our relationship was crazy from the start. We did not officially start dating until we knew each other for about a year. Our relationship started out as friends with benefits. We would hang out, sleep together, and even go on dates. Shim was deploying so he did not want anything serious. I knew I could stay faithful during his deployment. He did not agree, and after a while, we parted ways and did not speak for almost a year.

On the night he returned from deployment, he messaged me, letting me know he had gotten back. I went to visit him that night and the rest was history. We hung out every day, and became friends with benefits again for a few months. Around the second month or so, he finally asked me to be his girlfriend.

We were staying at a really nice hotel and it felt fitting for him. Shim never truly wanted to be in a relationship, and he told me that multiple times. Looking back now, I definitely should not have pushed him to change his mind as much as I did. Him not wanting a relationship and me pressuring him caused a lot of problems, but somehow, we worked.

When I first saw Shim, I was instantly attracted to him. He was the most attractive person I had seen in my entire life at that point. He thought the same about me and would give me compliments every day. In spite of our differences, I think our equal obsession about one another's appearances just helped our relationship work. Throughout our entire relationship we went through a lot. We dated for about seven months before he left on his first deployment. We were officially dating during this one. Before he left, we spent every second we could with each other. Looking back now, that was not healthy on our part, but like I said, we were obsessed. He had a room on base where he had his own room but shared a common area, so it was easy for me to stay over with him often. During our relationship, we went on many trips together. We went to Vegas, drove up North in CA, and I even met his family at one point. Our relationship somehow worked, but we were constantly fighting, breaking up, and getting back together. We had a lot of good times and a lot of bad.

When I went to visit him in Chicago, the trip was really fun, but sort of depressing. While he was at work, I was alone in our hotel room the entire time. I was depressed at some points during the trip, but it was a fun experience overall. We were able to do sightseeing every day when my boyfriend would get off work. He even got some time off during my visit. We went to the zoo, a museum, and took a boat tour around the city. We relaxed at the hotel a lot, went swimming, and spent some time in the hot tub.

Shim decided to make the best out of his time off work by taking some LSD. We had experimented with drugs together prior to this trip. Nothing too bad; just marijuana. Since I was leaving for OCS rather soon, I declined the offer to join him and his friends. However, I decided to stay with him to monitor them in case anything went wrong.

Since I studied his friends and their reactions to the LSD, and they all seemed fine, I did not think I would have an issue if I took a hallucinogenic drug just this once.

That decision would affect my life forever and change what might have been a bearable time at OCS into a real-life nightmare.

CHAPTER THREE

What is Psychosis?

Psychosis is something extremely hard to explain to someone who has never experienced it before. At least, not without scaring them. I have lost a lot of friends, potential boyfriends, and even relationships because I told them about my experience too soon. Psychosis is a sensitive subject. Looking back now, I know I should have waited, but their reactions could have been better as well.

If you've ever participated in a role-play video game like *Grand Theft Auto* or *Tomb Raider*, your character only making decisions and actions based on what button you pushed, you have an idea what it's like experiencing psychosis. Or, rather, your character does. It feels as if someone else is controlling your life and you are just there, living the situation. Except this experience was more like a nightmare I couldn't escape from. Every single one of your deepest darkest fears comes to life and you are seeing them and believing everything is true. Psychosis tricks your mind to believe everything you are experiencing is real and no one can prove otherwise.

Imagine watching a scary movie such as the *Texas Chainsaw Massacre*, and then think about experiencing those same thoughts and fears inside your brain and not being able to decipher if they are real or not.

My diagnosis over the years went between schizophrenia symptoms, psychotic features, psychosis, and bipolar with psychotic features. In the end, the determination was bipolar. My official diagnosis is bipolar, but that does not mean I will never relapse. My brain is still susceptible to psychosis, but with proper precautions, I will likely not have to worry about a relapse.

Psychosis is simply defined as an individual hearing or seeing things that do not exist, or believing things that other people do not. That is why psychosis can be so frightening, and I believe why people often misconstrue psychosis with schizophrenia.

This makes the experience much harder to explain because it's rare someone will understand what you were going through, unless they experienced it themselves.

There are many things that can cause psychosis; some of these include physical illness or injury. Experiencing abuse or trauma, using recreational drugs, consuming alcohol or smoking, and some prescribed medications have psychosis side-affects. Sometimes hunger and lack of sleep, spiritual experiences, and genetic inheritance can even play a factor.

What caused my psychotic break, however, was, regrettably, the use of marijuana and LSD. I say unfortunately because it was my choice to take drugs. It wasn't due to something out of my control like genetics; it was a split-second decision I made that sent me down the rocky terrain ahead.

CHAPTER FOUR

One Wrong Decision

July 2017

The night I took LSD is a night I will never forget. As I mentioned, I was visiting my boyfriend in Chicago, an unfamiliar environment, which might have made the experience worse.

I decided to take the acid because I thought it would not be scary. My boyfriend and his friends had taken some the day prior, and they all seemed fine and completely normal. It was inside a sour patch kid, so I did not know what kind of harm it could really do to my brain. I do not recall too much of that night, but I will try to recount as much as I can.

After we took it, we waited a bit but nothing happened so we decided to change and head down to the hot tub. It was hard to get down to the hot tub, because I started having large amounts of anxiety before we left the room. When we first started heading down to the hot tub, I began to cry out of nowhere and rushed back inside. My boyfriend came back to ask what was wrong, but then he saw me in distress. He calmed me down and then we left for the hot tub again and made it that time.

When we got to the hot tub, everything was fine for a little while but then more effects started to kick in and I began to see parts of the wall surrounding us coming off and floating around. We stayed for a little bit longer but then shortly after, we decided to leave and head back up to the room. Once we were inside the room, my situation got progressively worse. I am forever grateful my boyfriend had experience and was able to take care of me through the whole ordeal. If I had to choose, I would choose for it to have never happened but I am glad he was conscious enough to help me through that hard night.

Once we got into the room, I think he put the Jungle Book on to try and calm me, but it began to make things worse. My mind was far too gone. One of my very favorite shows back then and still to this day was *Friends*. I remember closing my eyes and seeing the complete series just flash in front of my eyes over and over again. I imagined as if I watched Friends over one-thousand times on repeat. My brain would not stop; it was going a mile a minute for over twelve hours.

At some point in the night, I made the mistake of looking at my eyes in the mirror. My pupils were almost as large as my irises, which freaked me out even more. I did not know what to do. I had never taken hallucinogenic drugs before, so I tried to make myself throw up multiple times in the hopes that I could expel the substance from my system. My boyfriend said that it was not going to help, and he was right, but I tried multiple times anyway.

I am not sure how we accomplished this, but at one point, we walked to Wendy's down the street to get some dinner because he thought that might help me get out of the bad trip. When we got back into the room from Wendy's, I still was not doing well. I stripped naked, wrapped myself in our bed comforter at one point, and laid there on our bathroom floor in the fetal position. I was screaming, crying, thrashing around and trying to get through the nightmare.

I thought I was going to die. A few times, I wanted to die because I thought that would be easier to deal with than the hell my brain was putting me through.

Around 4:00 or 5:00 in the morning, my boyfriend and I were lying in bed. He was cuddling me and I said something and then immediately heard my boyfriend get all excited because it was the first "normal" thing I had said in over twelve hours.

I felt weird; extremely drained, emotionally and physically, but got up and started eating the Wendy's we got the day prior because my stomach was growling. I ate, relaxed, and went back to sleep for a little while.

My boyfriend headed to work later that morning, and I relaxed, took a bath, and took it easy until he got off. When he got home, we went on a boat tour. That was the start of my recovery from the acid trip, and I left for Officer Candidate School (OCS) around a week later because I thought I was fine.

OCS was the start of my emotional unrest, which led to the worst turmoil filled three months of my life.

CHAPTER FIVE

My Breaking Point

August 2017

My memory of OCS is fuzzy at best. Sad to say, my psychotic break left me without much of my memories over a year-long span. I am not sure what triggered these episodes, but I do remember being at OCS for around two weeks, and I did not sleep almost the entire time.

As stated before, my father helped in my acceptance to OCS, which leads me into one of the manic issues I faced while attending the training.

One sign that someone is not doing well mentally is racing thoughts. Your mind is constantly thinking and going and will not let you rest. I experienced this phenomenon almost every night while attending OCS. I would lay in bed, attempting to sleep, but my mind was on a loop.

At OCS, they preached to us to be careful, wash your hands, do not touch your face, etc., because pink eye spreads like wildfire there. But my subconscious mind interpreted the statement in an incorrect manner. When the Officers told us pink eye spreads like wildfire, they would mention disease as well. This made me believe I was going to get sick and spread disease to all the other recruits, and be the cause of everyone's death. When I would try to sleep at night, my brain would repeat, "I am not supposed to be here", "my dad got me here", "I am going to get sick, get everyone else sick, kill everyone and be the downfall of the entire Navy". My brain would just speak these sentences on repeat, over and over until it was time to wake up … and then things seemed to be almost normal for the day. Until night fall when I would experience those racing thoughts again.

I do not know how I even stayed at OCS as long as I did. I will never understand how one person who did not sleep for two weeks could function in that type of environment for so long, but by the grace of God, somehow I survived long enough to be able to leave. I was even able to complete my swim qualification while in the weird mental state between reality and psychosis.

I am not sure what this mental state is called but, to me, it felt like I had tunnel vision and my head was cloudy. I have heard other mental health activists, such as Jesse Katches explain it as derealization. It feels as if you are disconnected from reality and in a fuzzy dream, but you are still aware enough to discern the difference between reality and a state of psychosis. I was able to be aware but uncontrollably terrified at the same time.

The Navy swim qualification test is not easy, even for those in a normal headspace. The swim test includes a deep-water jump, 50-yard swim, and floating for five minutes. Imagine standing on top of a high dive, already scared to death of everything around you and having to jump off in hopes that you have enough brainpower to get yourself back on top of the water.

I decided to go last, or almost last, because I was trying to prepare and calm myself down the best I could. When I got to the top of the high-dive, I was terrified but I took a leap of faith and attempted to finish my swim qual.

I survived the high-dive, and once I swam up to the top, I had to complete the 50-yard swim. Fortunately, you are allowed to complete the swim in any stroke you want, so I chose my favorite, the egg-beater, my strongest stroke. The eggbeater is a swim stroke commonly used in water polo, known to help propel swimmers in an upward direction. Somehow, I completed the swim and was not too terribly tired. The last task was what I was most scared about.

Prone floating is not just any normal floating. We had to "inflate" the makeshift uniforms they required us to wear somehow to utilize them as a floating device. The thought of having to do that was very scary. *How the hell am I going to complete this when I can barely function right now?* I thought as panic set in. I tried to stay as calm as possible. Once I got to the end, there was someone there talking people through how to inflate their clothes. I was able to inflate mine pretty easily and then I just floated there for five minutes, trying to relax as much as possible.

In spite of the fact I was not in the right mindset, I will forever be proud of myself for completing something that daunting while my brain was slowly failing me.

This accomplishment will always remind me that I can do anything I set my mind to (within reason). If I could complete a swim qual meant to be challenging, while my brain was slowly shutting down, then I can accomplish many great things.

I believe another thing that negatively affected me at OCS was the inability to form any friendships. I had roommates, but the majority of the time I saw them, we were studying, doing our hair, and going to sleep. I feel I freaked them out at some points, too, because I mentioned suicide, and was put on suicide watch. The main time you see anyone is at meal times, but that is more robotic than anything. You are not allowed to look at or speak to anyone; just have to focus on eating in the predetermined manner. Pick up the fork, place the food in your mouth, chew fully, put the fork down, and swallow before picking it up again. Although I know this method is supposed to teach discipline, it made it difficult for me to get enough nutrients to fuel my body and my brain for the day ahead.

The environment was not very welcoming. It is not supposed to be, but that did not help my mental state. The buildings and environment, to me, looked similar to a prison but without bars and high electrical fences. I am not sitting here bashing OCS and how they look. I am just stating that the environment did not help me kick myself out of the negative mental state I was experiencing.

I could sit here and say that I regret going to OCS or that I wish I could change it, but I do not. All I can do is learn from my experiences. I stand by the idea that everything in life happens for a reason. Maybe I was never meant to go to OCS in the first place, but the experience taught me lessons I will take with me for my entire life.

I learned that even when I am in a bad mental state, I can still complete a swim qualification, which means I am a decently strong swimmer.

Some other things I completed at OCS while in this mental state included drill and a physical fitness test (PFT). Drilling is pretty simple overall, but I was unable to catch on and struggled with drill throughout my entire time at OCS. The PFT is a little more involved and includes push-ups, crunches, and a 1.5-mile run.

By the end of OCS, in order to graduate, women aged 20-24 must complete 87 curl-ups, 39 push-ups, and finish the 1.5-mile run in 13:15 or under. The requirements to pass increase over time, but I was able to pass my first PFT with flying colors while also fighting a battle inside my brain.

Although I was not at OCS for very long, I am still proud of everything I was able to accomplish in the short amount of time I was there.

One good thing about OCS is that the program is voluntary. If it ends up being not right for you, you are allowed to go up to someone and tell them you quit. I had enough consciousness to be able to go up to an Officer and let him know it was just not working out for me anymore. I wish that had been the end of my struggle, but, alas, it was just the beginning.

The next couple of weeks at OCS were not as bad. I was not in training and being constantly yelled at, but I was still terrified of everything. One gentleman named Legman helped me out a lot at that time, and I am forever grateful for his generosity. I imagine with everything going on, I definitely freaked him out, but he was still extremely nice to me and I am glad I had him around. I hope he sees this someday and realizes I was not crazy but, yes, I was *going* crazy.

Psychosis is very similar to schizophrenia. I was experiencing schizophrenic symptoms while in psychosis, but that was not my official diagnosis. I recall hiding in my closet to call my mom where I decided to tell her what was really going on. I hid in my closet in fear that if someone heard me that I would get in trouble and get put in jail or some other horrible thing would have happened to me. This is where the schizophrenic symptoms come into play; I was extremely terrified of something that was not true and would not have happened but one-hundred percent certain it was going to, and no one could convince me otherwise.

Because I told an Officer I could not complete the program anymore, I was put into a holding group while waiting to transfer out and go back home. I did not expect my mother was able to come there, and I told her not to multiple times, but a few days after I confessed in the closet, she came and got me at OCS. Normally, it is not allowed for someone to leave without official discharge, but, under the circumstances, I was able to stay with my mom as long as I mustered and checked in every day.

My mom kept the real reason why I was going crazy a secret from the rest of my family, which I appreciate. This gave me the option to tell my family whenever I was ready to, and since the incident, I have told some, and others will find out when they read this book.

Instead of mentioning the drugs I took, my mom kept our family updated by explaining the entire situation as one huge anxiety attack, which it was, but in a much more dreadful way.

My mother stated in an email:

She thought she was going to be prosecuted for keeping things from the application process and go to jail for "lying on a federal application".

This statement was true; I had a constant loop of irrational fears circling inside of my head, with no way to stop it.

I will be forever grateful that my mom was able to come there for me, because I do not know what would have happened if she was not there. I also kind of knew she was coming before she left, because she accidentally sent a text meant for just my dad to our group chat. I had an idea that she was coming, but a few days later, I was surprised by my grandma as well.

My grandma and I have always had a pretty strong bond, so I am glad she was there as well. Below is my grandma's view of the situation.

Her mother was already there when I arrived. They had picked me up at the airport. She was extremely withdrawn from the world and did not want to do anything, and was rolled up in a ball on the bed. Her mother and I tried everything to bring normalcy back to her life by going out to breakfast, lunch, as well as touring a house in downtown Rhode Island. These were attempts to bring her out of a deep depression because she was severely detached from the world. She continually thought she was going to get her

*family and herself in trouble because she left
OCS. She was not allowed to be alone, so she
also went into the bathroom to have private
conversations with her boyfriend at the time.*

I do not remember much of that time, but I do think back
to the fact I thought I was going to get arrested because I was
not supposed to be there and my dad had helped me get into
OCS. And what would happen to him should I have been
considered AWOL? After I finally checked out and got my
DD214, we were able to go back home, but I still was not
convinced things were alright.

My mom was having a hard time, too. In another email,
she stated:

*Parenting sucks ass when your child, even at
23, is all the way across the country frozen in
fear and not even able to listen to simple
reasoning – not responding to questions on the
phone, sitting in a closet for fear someone's*

going to overhear our conversation, thinking
she's going to jail – all irrational but true to her.

I remember that phone call. I hid in the closet because I told my mom the truth about taking ecstasy a few weeks prior, and I did not want anyone to overhear in fear of getting in more trouble. Getting any words out at that point was hard. I was in the state of going between reality and psychosis. But that was one of the turning points in this unfortunate journey. I believe that conversation was what pushed her to fly out the next day.

Before my mom came to OCS, I had a conference call with my father and the XO on the base. I do not recall much of the situation besides sitting in a chair being frightened of what was going on around me.

This is the email Mom sent family members afterward:

A good update:
The XO of the program called Kevin and had
a conference with him and Erin this morning.
He explained a couple of things to her – she is
not in trouble. She does not have to follow the

OCS strict rules anymore, so there are no restrictions she was trying to self-impose. She will not have to pay the $3500 for uniforms she is not getting, and they are attempting to process her our ASAP by next week.

As most of you know, Erin was diagnosed with ADHD very young, and it has been under control without medication for more than a decade – to the point it's like she doesn't really have it anymore if that makes sense.

She has worked really hard to make that happen, but none of that really came up in her process to get in. It should have. She probably would have gotten a waiver, but it not coming up, among some other things, have caused anxiety for her. Anxiety that she "lied."

Her anxiety – evidently, it's something she has been able to control and be very high functioning without even Kevin and I realizing the extent of her anxiety. However, it just came to a head this week for various reasons.

37

She has not been believing Kevin and I that she was not in trouble. To be clear, it's not good this all happened like it has but she is not in trouble.

My mother and I both arrive today. She has been given permission to stay with us each night and through the weekend. Praise God!

Please continue to pray for her, and us.

Love you all!

I was still in constant fear when my mom arrived, and it definitely showed. Here are some of her accounts of that day.

Yesterday, I got Erin from base and being blatantly honest, it was hard. It was hard to see our daughter not act like herself. To have her get in the car and beg me not to drive off base for fear she was going to become a fugitive. But we did, holding her hand the whole time, and, of course, nothing happened.

Getting her to shower, getting her to put on civilian clothes, getting her to rest – all a struggle. It's a good thing I can be a strong mom when needed!

Anxiety and the fear that comes with it are powerful, but so is she, because even with all this fear and anxiety, she was able to do what she needed to do – request to DOR – and I'm thankful she did.

There are many other things she could have done – attempted to stick it out and get worse, hurt herself, or even commit suicide. Thank goodness for the Grace and Mercy and Protection we have all prayed for that kept any of that from happening.

For a long time, I didn't identify myself as a strong person, but reading my mom's words brought a tear to my eyes and made me proud of what I'd survived. I am glad I had the strength and consciousness to let an Officer know I couldn't continue at OCS. If I did not have the courage to do that, I fear for what might have happened.

When I dropped out, I walked into a random Officer's room and he was instantly agitated, because, in my fear, I was unable to address him correctly. His agitation did not sit right with me and I immediately began to shut down, whispering or talking under my breath, worried about speaking the words that would get me in trouble. I was completely terrified standing in a complete stranger's room, about to admit defeat. Somehow, I mustered up the strength to tell him I had given up and I no longer wanted to continue.

After I told him, there was a very short moment of relief, as if things might actually get better. Sad to say, that was not the case. I had hoped, prayed, and begged God for relief, every single day, but my conscious mind was starting to become a distant memory.

This was a hard time in my life, for everyone included, and, sadly, it was just the beginning. My mom did not know exactly what was wrong with me yet; no one knew, not even me.

The rest of my time at OCS was kind of a blur to me personally. I still did not shower much, which was not good because I had started my period. I continued to get a bare minimum amount of sleep. I was very afraid to be around other people, so I would often times not eat anything for a few days. Whenever I left my room at night I felt like I could hear and see things in the hallways. I saw dark figures that looked like tall, black demons. For a while, the majority of the most unpleasant things during my psychosis journey occurred at night. Eventually, the dreadful thoughts, feelings, and hallucinations completely overpowered my mind.

Friday August 18, 2017, my mom sent an exciting email to the family with the subject line, ERIN IS A CIVILIAN!!

It's over and done. Her DD214 is signed and complete. We have official originals.

Her discharge was "failure to complete commission". It's not dishonorable or a negative reflection in any way.

Long road ahead to recovery, but this is a great start!

Love to everyone!!

I know this made my mom very excited, but she was right; it was an extremely long road to recovery. I will have to fight every day to ensure I never relapse into psychosis again.

After I was discharged, we were on our way to the airport, I repeatedly said the FBI was after me and I was a wanted felon. What made this situation worse was that my gram truly got sick on her flight and fainted. I think they had to land early in order to tend to her, which I thought was my fault as well.

Everyone made it home safe. My mother and I felt things might have gotten better but sadly, they got worse.

CHAPTER SIX

Home, Not Healed

September 2017

When we arrived back home, I experienced more psychotic episodes.

I contemplated suicide at one point, for the second time in my life. I was alone in my room, writhing and holding my head. For one second, I looked down at my wrists and thought about slitting them, and then the thought left because I was no longer alone as I looked out my window and saw someone driving up our driveway. I believe it was my dad in his truck, but I am not certain. Without warning, I started crying for some unknown reason. I guess I was excited to know someone was coming home.

Here my mother accounts some of the experience.

We are officially home.

Today was very therapeutic for Erin – traveling with her seabag and not having it confiscated, not getting stopped by airport security, Diana not getting stopped, everyone making it home, and Kevin reviewing her DD214 with her have all been more concrete evidence it's all over.

Definitely more herself today than previously.

Continued prayers please – love to everyone!

I do not remember going over my DD214 with my dad. However, I do remember feeling a sense of relief every now and then, since I was still going in and out of awareness. But the whole ordeal was so overbearing, the only way my mind could handle things was to shut down. And when my mind would shut down, sadly, my memories were lost inside the chaos.

During my psychotic episode, I tended to see and hear things that weren't there. I believed I could talk to flies as well. I was afraid of everything and terrified of being alone. One significant moment was when I was pacing my room and throwing my head into my hands. It was during these few minutes I thought about suicide again. I glanced at my arms and wondered what it might be like to slit my wrists. Would dying hurt? Would it be more peaceful than the agonizing pain I was going through right now? Attempting to harm myself was heavily on my mind, but, thankfully, I was not alone for much longer before someone came home and snapped me out of it. This happened a few days before my boyfriend came out for a surprise visit.

My mother realized when I talked to my boyfriend that I acted somewhat normal. Unbeknownst to me, she planned with him to come and visit me for a bit to see if it would help. She told me multiple times that he was visiting, but I never once believed her until I saw him at the airport.

His visit, unfortunately, did not help much. I was too far gone at that point. We had some fun times while he was there, if you call spending hours at a hospital and watching him get surgery fun.

Apparently, he had a pilonidal cyst that had been bugging him for a while. When we went to the hospital, I swear we were there for eight or more hours. His numbing needle did not work very well, apparently, because he was in a lot of pain while they drained the cyst. He screamed a lot, and thrashed around. It was definitely a normal reaction. But I hid in a chair in the corner beyond freaked out about what was going on because, in my mind, I thought he was being killed.

One night while staying beside him in recovery, I woke up and turned the light on to watch the tv. I was watching *Jimmy Fallon*'s late-night show, but I believed I was really there in real life in the audience. When my boyfriend woke up and saw me, according to him, I was frozen and staring at the tv as if I was in a trance.

My boyfriend's visit was somewhat normal; he was able to bring out some regular emotions in me and at times, it seemed I was getting better. We were hanging out, going on dates, and acting as a normal couple during his visit.

We had sex a few times during his visit. That was fine, but I was menstruating at the time, which made me believe that I was being molested by the devil, because of the blood. I chose not to tell my boyfriend these thoughts. I felt it would have freaked him out. He believed I was acting normal throughout most of his visit. He had never been around someone in psychosis and I had never experienced it before either. I think we both tried to handle the situation to the best of our ability, even if that meant telling ourselves we were okay when we weren't.

Psychosis is a different experience for everyone. I never understood where my substantial focus on religious aspects during that time came from, but the doctors told my mother they probably originated from my normal life because I grew up going to church and believing in God. I credit most of my success in recovery to God and my faith in Him to heal my brain.

I do not remember much, but I cannot forget the flies used to "talk" about me behind my back, because I was not showering. I thought they kept tabs on me, which made showering harder because I always believed I was being watched.

And that wasn't even the worst of it. I had some very disturbing hallucinations. One of which was having to consume my own feces in order to save my father's life. He was sitting on a "throne" and I was laying under it. I will never understand why my brain made that one up. I figure it was another one of those "the Devil made me do it" scenarios.

A few days after these incidents, we were all heading out to dinner with my parents' friends who were in town visiting. Before we headed out, I was down in the horse corral picking up poop piles, one of my daily tasks, except this task had been much different lately. In real life, I was picking up piles of manure and stacking them into a barrel to be dumped. In my head, however, I was picking up piles of dead, poor, unfortunate souls and stacking them up in line to be tortured by the Devil. This was where my thought of serving the Devil originated from.

Then my boyfriend, mom, dad, sister, her boyfriend, and I all hopped into my dad's truck and headed to dinner. We were on our way to Seaport Village, which is near downtown San Diego.

This car ride was the defining moment in my psychosis journey.

I remember that I was sitting in the middle seat between my boyfriend and my sister's boyfriend. The sun was shining down at the perfect angle, which made it seem as if I was in

Heaven when I closed my eyes. I told my family I wanted to go into the light and my mom told me it was okay to, because she thought that it would have helped me. In my mind I felt as if I was letting go and dying. My mother told me when I opened my eyes that she could tell I was a completely different person, and I was.

Everything seemed to just instantly get worse upon arrival to Seaport Village. While we were getting out of the car, I told my mother I was afraid I would die because my phone battery was dying. She was able to talk me into the restaurant by just leaving my phone in the car.

Dinner was interesting. One thing while I am in psychosis is that I will eat anything, yet when I am of sound mind, I am extremely picky. When I order something, I usually make changes to it such as no lettuce or tomatoes, but I was too scared and unable to ask for those changes to the chicken tacos I got. I have no recollection as to why. I actually ate all of my tacos, which is surprising because I loathe tomatoes and my tacos had tomatoes all over them.

That wasn't the weirdest thing that happened that night either. I remember my boyfriend telling some story, and I perceived it as if it went on and on forever. Growing bored, I focused on some picture behind him, and my mind imagined we were in some saloon in the olden times. Except, instead of the usual fantasy most people experience, I *believed* we had travelled back in time.

When I had come out of that illusion, I was thrust into another, curtesy of my father's favorite show, The Walking Dead (TWD). The restaurant we went to was on a pier, so our chairs would rock back and forth from time to time, and all I could hear in my head was the snarling, hissing, and growling sounds the zombies made in TWD, which is weird, since I rarely watched it with him. In my mind, I felt like I was sitting on the top of a zombie pile that was rocking back and forth while zombies climbed up it and attempted to eat me. I had to sit there and try my hardest to act and look normal, hyper focused on my boyfriend, listening to his story and trying to forget all the terrifying things going on inside my brain.

Before we left that night, we all stopped at the bathroom. I remember being afraid of losing my dad, which was a common occurrence while I was in psychosis since he helped me get into OCS and every small thing made me think he was going to be taken away from me as a consequence of leaving prematurely. When he passed into the bathroom, I thought he was going into a maze and I was never going to see him again. He eventually came out of the "maze" and we all headed home.

Everything that happened after we got home is a blur. One distinct memory I have is going to a bar with my sister. We met our boyfriends there. A few bikers were surrounding pool tables, and, in my mind, I thought there was a huge bar fight and a bunch of people got murdered. I ended up telling my sister I was not feeling well and wanted to go home. She took me to her apartment before heading home, and when we pulled up and heard her dog barking in the window, it freaked me out. I literally thought her dog was going to eat me.

After some time, she took me back to my parents' house, and I do not recall much of what happened after that. I do know that my boyfriend was leaving the next day and her boyfriend brought him over so I could say goodbye. Except, I was so out of it that I never got to truly say goodbye. Things went dark after he left, and I do not have much more recollection of that night.

I remember bits and pieces of saying goodbye to my boyfriend. I do not know why I had to walk down to the end of the driveway, but I saw him and I was speaking nonsense. I faintly remember the look on his face. I could tell he was distraught, but I could not help the rubbish that was spewing from my mouth.

I very faintly remember the truck ride to the hospital. But I am very thankful they drove me to the emergency room that night.

Saturday, September 16, 2017, I was taken to the emergency room because the situation had gotten unpleasant.

We're at the ER. This particular hospital has an ER psyche team and separate psyche section of the ER.

Their psyche hospital is full (as they all are in San Diego) so where we go from here I don't know. She's just gotta get stabilized first.

The staff and nurses have been extremely comforting and helpful, reassuring us it's the right decision, which I know it is, but hard to fully accept.

We briefly saw the doctor, who gave her a shot of Zyprexa to get her to calm down and stop the anxiety psychosis loop of nonsense words coming out. He will be back at some point, along with a psyche liaison, who is a specialized psyche nurse, to start the eval process with information from us.

She's been pleasant – let them do her vitals, knew her name and birthdate, let them draw blood, and let them give her the Zyprexa shot with no issues. But she's also been crazy, running out of the bathroom pretty much in underwear only – poor security guard and Erin. That was stressful to say the least. Two nurses were immediately with me to help corral her.

She's now extremely tired and drowsy from the shot, which is great. She has not slept since Thursday night (neither have any of us). Kevin was in Denver until today when he flew back on short notice.

Our pastor is here, along with Diana. Tyler is with Shim and the dogs for the night and taking Shim to the airport later.

Please continue to pray for us. Especially Shim. He's pretty distraught, and not sure how to handle all this right now. He's been with us for almost 3 weeks trying to help her and then this happened out of nowhere yesterday and today. Saying goodbye to him to go to the hospital was quite traumatic for them both. Erin did not want to go, she did not want to leave him or the house, he did not want to let her go, but he needs to fly out tonight to get back to work and she needs to be here. We all know it's best.

On the way to the hospital, she sat in the back of the truck between Greta and Diana, holding both their hands and said a few times (in between tears and gibberish), "Thank you for taking me, thank you for taking me", so I know

54

she knows somewhere inside of her it's the right thing to do.

It's not easy. I feel like a failure. I'm lacking sleep but pushing through for now as we all are. Love you all, and please, please continue to pray. Doctors for wisdom, Kevin and I for discernment for decision making, Erin for peace at what's happening, and mercy and God's grace and healing power for us all. We gotta FIND HER, where she's lost, and GET HER BACK.

Love you!

Before I went into the hospital, I experienced a few hallucinations, including believing I was Jesus, talking to flies, and thinking that I was serving the Devil when I was performing specific tasks.

My brain was in turmoil, and while my family was driving me to the hospital, I was repeating the same things over and over again such as, "I'm Jake from State Farm, I'm Jesus," but there would be a few times I would break the cycle and I would thank them for helping me and taking care of me. My family told me all of this after everything was over.

Somehow, I ended up in the hospital. The first hospital I was taken to was a general hospital. They gave me some drugs to help calm me down and I was able to rest for the first time in a long time. I did not know how I ended up there. Now I know my family took me to ensure I was safe.

Taking me to the hospital was the right choice, but it was not the end. After my one-night stay in the general hospital, I was transferred to a mental ward, at the Balboa Naval Hospital. Eventually I recovered but I experienced a lot more hallucinations.

Ten days later, I had been checked into a psych ward at Balboa, a naval hospital.

When I was in the mental hospital, we had an outside area with some tables, chairs, and benches where we were allowed to hang out for outdoor time. One day, I was sitting outside at a table with a few other people around.

There was one gentleman lying down on a bench with a shirt covering half of his face, and I could only see one of his eyes. I thought that he was staring at me, so I looked back at him.

He suddenly turned into a wolf, jumped up, opened his mouth wide, and growled as if he was trying to kill me.

And I wholeheartedly believed he was going to.

Another recurring real-life nightmare I experienced while in the hospital was getting my "blood drawn". Now, to a person not experiencing turmoil inside their head, this statement may sound harmless, but, to me…

One of my favorite movies to watch was *Law Abiding Citizen* with *Gerard Butler*. There is one scene in that movie which always used to haunt me, whether I was in psychosis or not. The movie starts with two people breaking into a family's home then raping a man's wife and daughter and killing them. The man did not believe the law served justice to him and the situation, so he took things into his own hands after one of the two men was able to walk free. He tricked him into going to some remote location and ended up drugging him, strapping him onto a work table, and injecting him with morphine. He also kept the individual's tongue in place to keep the man from choking on it. After all of this preparation, the man looking for vengeance began dismembering the other's body one by one with different types of razors, saws, and knives, until he was fully dead and torn from limb to limb.

This movie was why getting my blood drawn made me fear for my life. Every time a doctor or a nurse told me I had to get my blood drawn, I would fear what happened to the man on that table was going to happen to me. I thought getting my blood drawn meant they were going to dismember me and my blood would be drawn all over the room.

I was not allowed to watch this movie while I was a patient, but the lighting at night would trigger the memories of that scene. While lying in my bed, the cheap light fixture would create an off-yellow rectangle reflection right above my bed. This was similar to the movie because he put a large mirror above the man so he was able to see everything being done to him. I could not sleep much during my stay at the hospital, until I started getting better.

Safe to say, I am still uneasy around off-yellow vintage lights.

I experienced a lot of different hallucinations and fears during my hospital stay.

One of the signs that I was not doing well was poor hygiene such as not brushing my teeth, or hair, and not wanting to shower. I am not sure where this hallucination came from, but this was common when I was taking a shower. I would look down at the drain and although it would look normal to others, I felt as if the drain was sucking me in and grinding me alive, sort of how wood chippers grind up tree parts. Almost the entire time I was in the hospital, I was afraid to shower. I would often take showers in my clothes because my aversion was so high. I have not shown any of these signs since I left the hospital.

Another disturbing thing I experienced during my stay at the hospital was catatonia. Catatonia is defined as an abnormality of movement and behavior arising from a disturbed mental state. Many doctors did not believe I was catatonic at first, but one nurse really fought for me. Her name was Amber and she was the key to my success, and my family and I will always be grateful for her.

Some of the catatonic symptoms I experienced were watching tv "frozen" in place. I would raise one of my arms with the remote and just stare at the tv. People would try to reach out to me but I could not hear them and was just stuck there. When my family would visit, we would play card games and I would freeze in place while putting my card down. I am sure the entire scenario was frightening for my family, but I do not have any recollection of those moments.

A lot of things happened during my stay. I flushed my clothes down the toilet and flooded an entire side of the hospital. I even played with my own feces. I do not like to talk about that, but it is true.

They had a phone in the hospital, so when I was doing better, I would call my family, and my boyfriend sometimes. I am surprised I even remembered the numbers, but I am glad that I did. Being able to talk to them really helped me in the situation.

When my mom sent this email the situation was slowly starting to get better, thankfully. With faith, family, and prayer, anything can happen.

Dear Family,

Thank you all for your continued love and support of us through this. Today is day 10 of Erin's time at Balboa Naval Hospital. There's that number again, 10 days. If you read my posts on Facebook you know 10 days is my hashtag to track my Erin posts. She was at OCS for 10 days and it changed her life. Now no matter how many sets of 10 days we need, she's going to get it back.

Yesterday, we met with her new doctor and it was a good meeting. I love when doctors try to manage you and they think you don't realize it. That is okay – the important thing is they HEARD us. Last Thursday was a good day, last Friday was NOT. The weekend was okay. Her new team has one doctor that was part of her old team, and he hadn't seen Erin since last Tuesday, until yesterday. Having the week break, he was expecting more progress, and he agreed she had moved backward, or at least not forward.

The medicine she first responded to so well in the ER was brought back over the weekend on an "as needed" basis, but yesterday we all agreed they would actually make it her main medicine and wean her off the one we ALL now agree she's simply not responding to. Her sleep is restful and solid 9-11 hours most nights, and consistent when she has the medicine that's working.

Yesterday, our time with her was wonderful. She ate all her dinner, had complete and coherent conversations, logical and linear thinking, and many times if she said something that did not make sense, she stopped and said, "That doesn't make sense". We also played one of her favorite games – Last Word. We left early because one of the nurses, "Mama T", was starting an arts/crafts time and she seemed very interested to go. It's important we see her, but she has another week or so there (and maybe longer) and she needs to bond and interact with her fellow patients. It also made goodbye pleasant, not tearful and not filled with her saying, "Please take me home."

This morning, my phone check with the nurse confirmed she's much like she was yesterday, so more stable, good sleep, ate breakfast, meeting with the doctor, and then going to art therapy. I'll call her around 10am to visit with her.

Every day is a struggle, for us, but SO MUCH for her.

On Saturday, she called me, "mom, mom". It's a specific way she has always said it and I hadn't heard it since before she left for OCS. When I first brought her home from OCS, I told Kevin when I hear her call me "mom, mom", I'll KNOW she's on her way back to us. A true gift from God to hear her call me that Saturday.

The doctor yesterday gave us great hope this is a temporary diagnosis of psychosis brought on by an underlying mood disorder, not permanent psychosis. It so happens the antipsychotic they have her on now, after the changes, serves both purposes. It helps break psychosis and regulate mood disorder. She also said don't get concerned about her needing to be on medicine for life, because she may or may not need it.

Please pray for her to continue to relax and her brain to heal. Medicine and therapy and treatment are ALL part of God's plan but her healing truly lies in Him.

Blessings and love to you ALL!

Love,

Allison, Kevin, Greta, and Erin

I cannot place that interaction with my family before I lost almost all of my memories. But when my mom stated I had said, 'that doesn't make sense', I suddenly remembered the scenario where I had said that. Some memories are slowly returning, but I do not believe I will ever fully get them back.

On September 29th 2017, my family was visiting me and they were able to see something they had not before.

Dear Family,

Our visit with Erin Thursday afternoon was very informative because we actually observed her slip away from us into catatonia psychosis and then we watched her medicine take effect and she came back out of it. There was a significant shift of reality vs non-reality. It was the last bit of observation her treatment team needed to make the decision for her medicine regimen today and hopefully to remain for the future.

Today – 90% clear day!!! Small things happened – she made her bed unassisted and without prodding.

She showered, unassisted and without prodding. All her clothes were on correctly all day. She had logical reasons for not doing certain things, such as not washing her hair because she doesn't like their shampoo and wants us to bring hers. She attended community group and art group on her own and participated. She remembered meeting with her doctor, knew her nurse's name, what month it was, that tomorrow is Saturday, the time, etc. Yesterday, she attended Spirituality Group and was able to participate and talk about everything with her nurse, re-explaining it all in a way that made sense to her.

The more days like this, the better. They have goals for her to attain, aside from her psychosis being clear, before she should come home (such as all the things I listed above).

We also found out she can (most likely) continue out-patient treatment there even though she is not active duty. For the purposes of health-care, she is still considered Kevin's dependent because we pay for Tricare for her. The reason they will make an exception for her is due to her case being an abnormal case for them, and an abnormal case in general. Balboa is a teaching hospital and their mental health cases are mainly depression, suicide prevention, and PTSD, so she is an interesting case for them. I know it might sound weird to say it that way, but it's reality. For her, it provides continuity of care and we won't have to start from scratch with another set of doctors.

She took a nap today. It's the FIRST nap she's taken since she came home from OCS on 8/20. It's a small accomplishment, but a giant step toward recovery. It means her mind is finally relaxing enough to truly rest and quiet enough to sleep, instead of just being sleepy from medicine.

Please pray Saturday is another clear day, with healthy vitals, and she continues progress toward self- care.

Much love and blessings to everyone!

That was the first day in over a month I had felt good and right-minded. For the first time in a while, I wanted to do those things. I wanted to shower and make my bed. That switch is fascinating, to go from not wanting to shower, brush my teeth, get dressed, and just not wanting to do anything, and then one day waking up and feeling good enough to finally be able to do life's daily simple tasks.

My mom stated they saw me switch between psychosis and reality. It is hard to understand how the switch can happen so fast and drastically. One day, I am fighting a battle in my mind I believe I will never get out of then the next day life is back to normal and I can finally decipher reality from fantasy.

Psychosis is basically an elongated, horrendous panic attack. I do not wish psychosis upon anyone, even my greatest enemies. Those three months were the worst parts of my life. Imagine experiencing some of the most frightening things you have ever seen inside your mind, and not being able to tell yourself it is not real.

Most of the things I did while in psychosis I didn't have much control over or memory.

CHAPTER SEVEN

Recovery on the Horizon

October 2017

After that first day of doing simple tasks without much prodding in the hospital, things started to progressively improve. On October 2nd of 2017, my mom sent a cheerful email to my family informing them all of the great progress I had made.

> *Dear Family,*
>
> *It's all very good news for Erin at this point. Today I still cried, but mainly happy tears full of thankfulness and praise for her healing and recovery. Your prayers have truly buoyed us through this entire process, and medicine, doctors, good nurses and techs, and God's*

amazing healing have all brought our daughter back to us. I have felt so desperate and faithful at the same, resting in God's grace that is deeper than I could ever fully imagine until now, and I'm positive it is even deeper than I know.

She will be coming home within the next couple of days. The only reason I can imagine she'll be there this coming weekend is if they still need medicine fine tuning.

This weekend the nursing staff did another "positive challenge" with her anti-anxiety medication with one of her "as needed" doses. Since we were there for a longer period of time, it allows us to give feedback and be involved in seeing how she responded from our POV. Every positive challenge has manifested great results - meaning her mind CLEARS with the anti-anxiety medicine.

This is further proof catatonia is the culprit.

This morning was her CLEAREST morning and so they are changing her anti-anxiety meds

70

to three times per day scripted (that's how they did it over the weekend for the challenge) and lowering her anti-psychotic by 25%. She is still very low dose as well, for everything.

Catatonia can be induced or made worse by antipsychotics. Erin is the clearest when her anti-anxiety meds are the highest in her system (later afternoon/evening), and the least clear when her antipsychotic is the highest in her system (morning), so the medicine change should fix this to where she can be clear all day.

If tomorrow morning goes well again then eventually she will come off the antipsychotic completely. If it doesn't go well, they will leave her medicine as it has been.

It's all complicated, but very interesting.

Tonight, OUR daughter was back. It was wonderful and amazing. And she also had her MRI done. This is to rule out any organic causes, which we are not expecting, but still need to be ruled out.

Pray her medicine fine tuning works and her mind remains clear and rested. She actually asked us to leave a little early tonight – she wanted "personal rest time" in her room to read and relax before bed.

We were fine with that – it sounded exactly like something the Erin we've known for 23 years would say.

Much love and blessings to you all!

I remember bits and pieces of that day. I was finally feeling clear and knew the fiasco was almost over. I remember my mom rolling me in a wheelchair to the back in order to get an MRI. I was still really scared throughout the process, but I stayed strong and was able to get through the procedure. On October 4th it seemed things were finally getting better.

Thank you all for your emails and prayers. I feel we're in the final stretch! She sounded so good this morning – clear and positive – and had a good night of sleep.

They might be transitioning her to the "step-down" facility today. This is the next step toward her coming home. It's more freedom, and less restrictive.

It also means they're probably not going to be adjusting her medicine again, but Kevin and I are meeting with the doctor team tomorrow and will find out. Her medicine can continue to be adjusted as an out-patient.

Of course we want the transition to happen, but in the right timing so there's no relapse. Please continue to pray for us all to stay on the right course and not get ahead of ourselves as well.

God's timing!

Blessings and love

A few days later, things were looking promising for me to be released on the following Friday.

Erin was transitioned to the step down. She was very excited. There's a good chance she can come home Friday.... please pray that's the right thing to do.

I don't want our very human parental desire for her to come home to interfere with the BEST mental health care choice for her. The move to a new unit caused a little anxiety for her, which is very normal for Erin. The anxiety is due to her wanting to come home and the fear it may not happen. The new unit is also very quiet, not as structured, and a change – but she has to manage this well enough to prove she's ready.

We don't want her to come home early and relapse, but they're not going to completely fix 23 years of how she responds to anxiety while she's there. That's going to happen during outpatient cognitive behavior therapy, along with continued medicine.

Please pray she continues to maintain how well she is doing and works on managing her anxiety tonight, tomorrow, and tomorrow night.

Two nurses from her old unit came over to meet with us during visiting hours. They are very happy with her progress, but also cautiously optimistic about her leaving Friday.

Much love and blessings

My case was a lot different than the doctors and nurses at Balboa had seen. I was their first psychosis/schizophrenia brought on by illicit drug use case, and I believe I left an impact on every single one of them.

It was October 5th 2017, and my mom sent a great news email to our family. I was going home the next day. The whole affair was finally over and it was time for healing to begin, or so they thought.

She's coming HOME tomorrow.

We had a meeting, her included, with her treatment team. She was fully involved and understood her diagnosis, medicine she's taking and why, and the plan for when she gets out. It was a great meeting. Praise God for healing and modern medicine!

The doctors and nurses have all been quite happy with her progress this week. A little surprised, actually. We are not – standing in faith!!

She will not be seen at Balboa for follow up because she is not active duty and they do need to prioritize them. They strongly encourage we take her to the UCSD CARE program, which is a cutting edge, wrap around care (including things like preparing to enter the workforce) and integrated mental health program between psychiatry and psychology. We will start that process tomorrow. They will provide a link for UCSD to download her medical records. Her diagnosis is catatonia, currently unspecified. She will continue to take her current medications for the foreseeable future, and a diagnosis will be outpatient with any medication changes as needed.

None of the doctors feel she will need medication forever.

Also, she did share with me the other day what happened at OCS – she said the constant yelling was just too much, yelling at her and everyone having to yell everything back. She said her brain just shut down because she could not handle it – and that is okay – it's not for everyone. Then things just got worse from there. We are so happy for her healing and the care she has received at Balboa.

Thank you for all your love and prayers. Today in the meeting she told the team she was blessed and lucky to have such a loving and caring family, and she knows many people do not have that.

Being in the hospital was traumatic, but it was essential to my recovery. I had still been experiencing catatonia and hallucinations but the team was working daily to bring me back to my normal self.

Leaving the hospital was a little upsetting. It had been my safe space for almost three months. Getting back into the normal routine of life was something new and scary. It was a little upsetting that I was not able to be treated as an outpatient there. But I did not need to stay and they were happy I recovered well enough to move on. The care program I was accepted into was exceptional and key to my recovery.

My family's and friends' prayers had been answered. I was free of psychosis and finally had a clear brain. My first week at home was great and it seemed a great recovery was on the horizon.

Erin's first week at home has been really good. She's returned to the gym, getting really good sleep, not driving yet but up and about actively doing things everyday with Diana and our family. She's also worked on her resume some and is looking for jobs she might want to do in the future. For the most part, the Erin we knew for 23 years is back, and, most importantly, her mind is clear. She's positive and toward the end of this week is feeling better (physically) and beginning to accept the reality mental health care is a new normal for her. One of her medicines was also lowered and she's had a positive response to that change.

Surprisingly, and I say that word not in a negative way, her boyfriend has remained involved and supportive. I say "surprisingly" simply because mental health is all new to him – he's young like her and doesn't know what he doesn't know. Whether they last for the long haul is yet to be seen, but for now, he's a source of love and support.

Today was her first appointment at the UCSD CARE center. It was a great experience. Her psychiatrist could not have been hand-picked to be a better fit (praise God!). Erin immediately clicked with her, and it was a 2-hour intense "interview" intake visit. Kevin, Diana, and I were all involved at different times. She will be going to a once-a-week young adult group therapy, once a week Psychiatry session, and once a week individual therapy session.

What I didn't realize is UCSD CARE is solely focused on psychosis mental health care. Their age group is teen to young adults under 30, and those with a first Psychotic break within the last 2 years of seeking treatment there. It's highly specialized and focused care for Erin's very specific age group and needs. All of this is truly amazing, and we all feel blessed to have this care available to her. For me, personally, I feel hopeful and at peace more than ever for her long-term success.

We also learned today the idea therapy is "not-beneficial" for psychosis is true to an extent with normal outpatient therapy, but this UCSD program has a therapy program specific for psychosis. It will be interesting to see how it's different than the therapy we've had experience with over our lives.

One of the medicines she's on, her antipsychotic, does have weight gain and diabetes as a side effect. It's due to metabolic and hormone changes that even if she eats really well and exercises all the time are still a problem. It is good for acute care, not long-term care. It's the one that was lowered earlier this week and she will be weaned off, but it's a process. Erin is by no means fat, but she has gained some weight, so the doctor prescribed an anti-diabetes medicine for the short term to counter these side effects while she is weaned off.

The new psychiatrist reiterated what all the other doctors have said; it is highly unlikely this is schizophrenia or a schizo-affective disorder. This is good news for many reasons. We were also reminded again today by this doctor, after our interview time with her, how Erin was truly suffering and very, VERY sick. Kevin and I no longer feel any guilt for taking Erin to an inpatient facility – that has been a process to work out, and not easy. It is now clear it was the only choice to save her, to find her again and bring her back to us.

The doctor also explained stress and anxiety do not "normally" cause a Psychotic break, UNLESS someone has a vulnerability to it and then yes it most definitely can. This, more than anything, makes sense when I look back on all the major life events we dealt with in our lives since May – stress and anxiety were alive and well for all of us – and Erin was absorbing so much of it, not realizing how it was affecting her.

Please continue to pray for her, for us, for wisdom of her new doctors and positive outcomes for her new therapy program, medicine weaning and adjustments, and for Diana while she is here being a source of physical, mental, and emotional help and support.

Faith has been our rock, and I cannot imagine this journey without it or ALL your prayers and love. We are blessed and loved to have such a wonderfully supportive and involved family, even from afar.

We're all feeling positive about the future.

Sadly, on October 20th 2017, I had a relapse and my mom sent an update to the family.

Dear Family,

It is with a very heavy and worried heart, I say Erin had a set back and relapsed into psychosis again. She is not going in-patient again as of now, but reality is if some forward progress is not made over the weekend and Monday, by Monday evening or Tuesday, she could be. Please pray this is not the decision we are facing on Monday afternoon.

Lowering her antipsychotic last Wednesday was most likely the beginning of this happening, and just to note, it was not the choice of her new psychiatrist, but her other one from the hospital and in response to our worries about some side effects (weight gain and metabolism). It is also a mood stabilizer as well, and there is now no doubt her psychosis is due to a mood disorder. Even though she is in psychosis again, truly, for the long run, a mood disorder origin is a great prognosis for long term success. (That's me trying to stay positive in the face of despair right now...)

Right now, her medicines have been increased for two reasons – to break through the psychosis and provide sleep. The psychiatrist was adamant again today, several times, how important sleep is to her recovery. She did not sleep well on Monday due to her mania episode starting that day, and neither she nor I got much,

*if any, sleep Wednesday night. The psychiatrist
also took some time today explaining how
   she feels about medicine; in particular, the
anti-anxiety one Erin is on, due to its long-term
side effects (mainly addiction). She's extremely
conservative and cautious, meaning if she's
prescribing a small increase, it's because her
level of concern for Erin's health warrants it.
She also preferred to increase her anti-anxiety
at night to help Erin sleep vs adding any more
medications or a sleep aid. Too many medicines
become problematic.*

*Her psychiatrist is markedly concerned, so
much so she called me back into the session at
the end to clarify again the medicine changes,
plan of constant supervision and monitoring at
home, and to inform me what she would be
suggesting Monday if some forward movement
wasn't made. Monitoring includes blood
pressure/pulse/food and fluids. Even though I
hate that Erin is in psychosis, it was good for*

diagnosis purposes, and other reasons. Both her doctors were able to see her varied mood levels (normal last Friday, mania Monday, psychosis today) to get the overall scope of what we've seen.

Both her doctors were able to fit her into their schedule twice next week, plus group therapy. We are so grateful for this program and the support they are offering.

Some good news – she did have a wonderful experience Monday in her group therapy, and the psychologist shared with us today Erin was expressing a great deal of insight, and willingness to share.

Both very good. Her individual therapy is with the same doctor who leads that small group. Both doctors also said her response to medication is good for the long term because so many patients do not respond to medicine as positively as she has.

Right now, this is terrifying. I'm trying, we're all trying, to hang on to that string of hope, but it's not easy. We need prayer, and she needs prayers for healing and a miracle turn around this weekend. She woke up this morning and said to me, "Mom, please help me get out of psychosis tonight at bedtime." She told me, "Mom, I think you're having an episode". I agreed with her and said I was having an episode worrying about my daughter, and she said, "I'm worried about her, too."

I recall bits and pieces of this time.

For example, I was outside shoveling horse manure and Gram was with me. Our horse Rex knocked over the handle to the wagon we used to fill up, and I stated, "The devil made him do it." While I was in psychosis, a lot of my hallucinations included religion, which means this proclamation was concerning. Woefully, I was admitted to the hospital again.

Dear Family,

After the two doctor appts today, it was decided the best place for Erin was the hospital again. Truly for her utmost safety and any medicine changes. Not what anyone wanted but reality nonetheless.

By the time she was admitted through the ER, which took from 4:30pm-10pm, it was bedtime in the unit so we said goodbye at the door, and that was not easy. However, the night shift greeted her with loving and welcoming arms, and that was comforting for Kevin and me.

The nurse said, "Do you remember me, Erin? I sing to you every morning." I can never truly express the angst and uncertainty we all feel. There are no words, but there are also no words to describe the comfort and peace we feel, at the same time, knowing she's being taken care of in an environment that is safe and loving.

Please continue to stand in faith and prayer with us as we need it now more than ever.

Being in the hospital the second time was hard. My mom thinks it was because I knew I was in the hospital this time. My recovery was quicker this time, because I remember going home on Halloween.

Dear Family,

Erin is making progress, but it is slower and different than last time. She knows she's in the hospital (last time she wasn't very aware of that until closer to the end) and that is both a positive and negative. Positive because she's advocating for herself more and wanting to do things to get home. Negative because she's so focused on wanting to come home, leaving her there is hard on her ("please don't leave, please stay, please take me home") and it's causing angst that manifests itself in various ways.

This weekend will be important toward getting her home because they made some medicine adjustments that we all hope move her toward the coming home goal.

Specific prayer requests – clearing mind, less confusion, and more self-directed and initiated self-care (showering every day on her own, eating and drinking enough on her own, other good personal hygiene on her own).

Trying to rest my mind in the positive, I've gone ahead and scheduled an appt with her outpatient psychiatrist for 11/6, and she will go to group therapy before.

Much love and blessings to all. Thank you for standing in faith and prayer with us.

Self-care was a constant issue while I was in psychosis. Not wanting to shower, brush my teeth or hair is a sign that I may not be doing well.

Dear Family,

I thought I'd start with specific prayer requests first:

(1) Her mind to continue to clear and more rapidly

(2) Agitation level to go down

(3) Positive response to the medicine change happening today

(4) More positive attitude

Tomorrow will be a week she's been in the hospital again. Her recovery seems slower than we'd hoped and different this time. I'm actually not sure it's slower. I think we just wanted it to be quicker... but I don't know.

There is definitely a more negative outlook from her this time because everything is about getting to go home – literally everything – instead of focusing on getting clearer. It's just, "I want to go home." Trying to explain the clearer mind means going home, and that should be her focus, is difficult.

When I say everything is related, I really mean everything – "yes, let's play Farkle because when we're done, I get to go home with you," or, "yes, I'll eat my chicken because when I'm finished, I get to go home with you," or, "mom,

I'm going to beg you, please let me go home with you..." and so it goes and goes and goes, our whole visit, to the last goodbye for the night. Sometimes we have to laugh about how she connects everything to this – to remain sane if for no other reason – because her connections are clever, showing thought process and linear thinking.

It's not easy and I can't fully describe how crappy this all is – let's just say sleep is currently not my friend, or eating (hey, I'm losing weight!). It's hard on all of us – Kevin, Greta, and Diana as well – and we all process it differently, but we're hanging in there as a team.

Even though she asks to go home all the time, because she is not demanding to leave, she is still on voluntary hold. If Erin were to get aggressive or demanding about leaving that would change to involuntary for 72 hours because she still needs the safe environment.

Some progress is definitely happening – self-directed self-care (hygiene, appearance) for example. I never realized how important a "marker" self-care is in relation to mental health – not having the desire or initiative to do it yourself is a flag.

It's not like we personally care if she looks clean and dresses properly, but it's a daily goal she must achieve.

She also called me yesterday. When she's not clear, she calls me on HER cell phone (not mine) and even though that's what she did yesterday, it's still progress because it's the first phone call she's initiated this time. Everything that moves her toward self-initiating more normal things is good.

Last night as I was leaving, one of the active-duty techs (corpsman) pulled me aside to share a sweet story about a conversation Erin initiated with him. He's young – maybe her age – she asked him when he thought her psychosis was going to go away because, "I just can't catch a break." It was the first time (this time) he felt she was able to have a clear conversation with him for a period of time. He said it made him tear up, to see her making progress, and how she's so sweet natured and sometimes funny. We are very blessed and thankful for the care and love she is receiving at Balboa Naval Hospital. Truly we are. There's definitely hope in the midst of despair, just needing a little more hope these days. Pray we see some more today.

Some of the scenarios my mom mentioned I do remember. I cannot recall a specific scenario, but I recall mentioning multiple times that I wanted to go home and doing specific things would make going home happen. I was on the road to recovery and things were looking up.

CHAPTER EIGHT

Recovery in Sight

November to December 2017

On November 1st 2017, my mom sent an update to the family about my little bit of time at home.

> *Dear Family,*
>
> *Erin came home Halloween night (last night), and we're all happy she's home.*
>
> *It's all different than last time – she's a little depressed (her words), more overwhelmed and very tired, but she's home and happy to be here. No one really knows how psychosis works, or affects the brain – this is according to her doctor- and after going through this twice now,*

I would concur. However, just watching her, it's like the world gets blocked out, so when she starts to clear, it all comes rushing back to life and she gets overwhelmed. Of course this is just my observation... no one knows, and she explained that finding the words to describe what's happening in her brain during psychosis is impossible.

She's very, very tired – please pray she continues to sleep as much as possible to fully recover, that it's restful, and her therapy and other doctor appts are a source of comfort and steps toward success. She meets with her therapist this week and is starting group therapy and seeing her psychiatrist next week.

Thank you for continuing to support us with your love and prayers.

Two days later, it was November 3rd 2017 and I had been doing well.

Dear Family,

Erin had her first therapy appt today after this hospital stay, and Dr. Mirzakhanian said Erin is doing well overall and where she expected Erin to be, in a good way.

Two weeks ago, today, we were in her office with the onset of psychosis, trying to determine if she needed to be in the hospital, and now we were there with Erin in recovery. It's easy to forget how quickly this has all happened, but it's a good reminder to be grounded and realistic about expectations, for us and especially for Erin about herself.

She has more appts and group therapy next week.

Please continue to pray for Erin to recover, sleep, manage her feelings of being overwhelmed, and communicate so we make sure a relapse doesn't happen. To say I'm currently gripped with a fear she's gonna relapse again is a serious understatement. I'm sure my fellow psychosis teammates – Kevin, Greta, and Diana – feel the same, although I'm maybe a little more neurotic. ;-) Literally everything becomes a question of, "Is it happening again?" Because it can happen so rapidly, and it's hard to not let that feeling from us overwhelm her.

Luckily for my mom and the rest of my family, it is September of 2022 and I have never relapsed into psychosis again. I have had issues with anxiety, panic attacks, and some other occurrences but never psychosis – I will go into details of those other issues later.

It was November 14th, three days after my parents' wedding anniversary and two weeks after I had come home, and my mom sent another good update to my family.

Dear Family,
Thank you for continued prayers. Erin is doing really well.

Today is 2 weeks since she came home from the hospital and a milestone because last time we did not make it this far and she relapsed.

Both doctors are pleased with her progress and support her plan, which is:

Start volunteer work soon, then move into part-time or full-time work in the New Year.

There are continued challenges ahead and need for specific prayers:

1. Her doc is continuing the weaning her off the anti-anxiety medication and wants her completely off in 1-2 months from now. We start another step-down today. Last week's step-down had no negative side effects and we pray it's the same this week.

2. Looking ahead, there are definite side-effects the anti-anxiety med balances out from her anti-Psychotic med. As the anti-anxiety is lowered, how/when/if will the anti-Psychotic be lowered as well. Please pray for this transition ahead so it can go smoothly and everyone, including her doctors, are guided in wisdom.

3. Part of lowering her anti-psychotic is adding in a mood stabilizer, because, ultimately, that mood stabilizer keeps triggers away. If the triggers are managed, then no psychosis. Pray for this transition as well – it's going to start soon (I think the next visit) because the Doc gave us options to consider and choose one.

4. Erin's participation in group therapy. She needs to attend, and she is, but not diving in to claim it as her own and really participating. She's not always been a "joiner" but this is an important group for her to attend weekly. She needs wisdom and guidance from others in her group, but she also needs to learn to be that to others – honestly, the latter is where she will grow the MOST in her journey. She has already proven her ability to do this based on unsolicited feedback from her fellow in-patients. Her unabashed honesty and willingness to share without concern of judgement is a strong example to many. She does not realize the positive affect she provides by doing this naturally, or how hard it is for people to do what seems so easy for her. Pray she learns to use this to help others and not be self-focused.

5. Side effects. All medicines have side effects..... the most worrisome to Erin right now is weight gain. Pray for this to all even out.

6. Her boyfriend is coming to visit the day after Thanksgiving. Pray it's a good visit for them both, and for him to continue to be a source of patience and understanding. So far, long distance, this has all been in place from him already, so we all hope that continues in-person.

7. Diana's leaving. Eventually, it's going to happen. She has to get back to her normal life. Erin has to manage on her own, and so do we. She's been a tremendous presence of support for us all over the last 2 months, but the support is/was to help Erin transition and stabilize-

having her leave means that is happening, but it's still hard to think of it happening. We have a few weeks until it does. Pray it all goes smoothly!

Blessings and love to everyone. We feel your support and prayers from afar and continue to need them every day! We are so thankful.

I do not remember much of Thanksgiving, and I forgot my boyfriend came for a visit. Psychosis was a traumatic brain experience (TBE), and I will live with the effects forever. Unfortunately, my boyfriend and I did not last much longer after this. We had been doing well, but I can only conclude he couldn't forget everything that happened. He was too traumatized, and I completely understood.

It was November 28th, and my mom sent her second to last email to all of our family.

Dear Family,

Hope all of you had a wonderful Thanksgiving! Our family time was relaxing and filling. Plus, we started Christmas decorating.

It's been a while for an update and that's because Erin is doing really well. Every day gets better and she continues to make progress toward her goals of driving and job!

Some specific prayer requests:

Job – She's working hard toward this, and has a job interview this Thursday! It's a part time position at San Diego State University as an Admin Asst to the professor who runs The Math Learning Center. Honestly, the pay is not great, BUT the hours are. It's entry-level into a University system that has great benefits (even for part time employees). She can take the trolley to save time and gas, and it doesn't start until late January so she would have more time to continue to improve. Please pray for a positive outcome and for her to have confidence for this interview.

Driving – this is very dependent upon her medicine levels. Please pray she continues to have success toward this goal.

Medicine – so far, all her side effects have been very minor (mainly restlessness), and addressed by simply switching the order of her medicine in-take. The mood stabilizer was added, and she chose to try Lamictal. It has the least side effects and drug interactions, but the one very serious side effect possibility is a rash called Stevens Johnson Syndrome. It's rare, and very dangerous (not gonna lie...), but always a possibility. Please pray she continues to have success toward long term medicine management, and no rash symptoms or problems.

Diana – she is returning to TX Saturday. Please pray for safe travels and a smooth transition for us once she leaves. The support she has provided while here is indescribable. It's been a true blessing.

Today is 4 weeks since Erin has been home after her relapse. Mine and Kevin's fears of another relapse continue to fade every day, but I would be lying to say there's not always a gnawing feeling of "what if" in the back of my (our) minds.

Erin is very good about filling out her daily journal and the questions she answers helps us to monitor her without intrusion. IF anything were to happen again, this daily journal is a good place to track any changes I'm thankful she's diligent about filling it out.

Blessings and love to you all! Your prayers, support, and love are all felt and appreciated. This entire ordeal has proven how blessed we are for the love and support of family and friends.

As stated before, it has been almost five years to this day that I have not relapsed and gone back into psychosis. I know my parents do worry but I hope they still do not constantly fear of a relapse since I am doing very well. On December 15th 2017, my mom sent her last email to our family.

Dear Family,

Hope your holiday season is going well. So far it is here in San Diego!

Erin found out today, when the HR department for San Diego State University called her, she officially got the job as Admin/Office Manager for The Math Learning Center with Professor Bowers. She will start second week in January at 20 hours per week, and will take the Trolley to avoid university traffic and parking.

She is doing really well these days. The first weekend Diana was gone was a little hard on all of us, but it was the right time for her to go so Erin could start moving toward independence, and she has. Her anti-anxiety medicine is continuing to be lowered, and now she is only taking a very low dose at night. Eventually, it will be gone because she was not prescribed this medicine for anxiety. Its main purpose was to counteract her catatonia symptoms of psychosis, and to help with some (minor) side effects of her antipsychotic medicine.

Since it's reduced to zero during the day, she started supervised driving this week. It has been a long time since she drove, so Kevin and I felt a week of supervised driving was a good start. Today, she drove solo for the first time, and I know it felt good for her!

One of her good friends was back in town visiting, and she spent the day with her, then went to her therapy appointment solo for the first time, and tonight went downtown to a country bar to hear a band play and do some line dancing.

Please continue to pray for her to respond positively to her medicine changes. So far NO negative side effects to any changes, and she shared with us she no longer has racing thoughts all day. At first, I know this felt weird to her, but now she knows what it's like to NOT have them, and she understands how they were negatively affecting her before, absorbing so much of her time and life.

Through all this, we have prayed she would be the "same Erin" who came back to us, just better – a stronger person emotionally and mentally, healthier mind and outlook, more in control of her emotions instead of them controlling her, and a person not ashamed or afraid of her struggle. So far so good with all of this.

Thank you for continuing to pray with us and for us.

She will be visiting Austin 12/28/17 so I hope whoever can see her will.

I do not remember visiting Texas on or around December 28th, 2017. I am sure I did but I do not know for sure.

CHAPTER NINE

Sharing My Story

One of my goals in life I always try to implement is being nice to those around you. You never know what someone is going through, so it is best to always try and be positive because you will leave an impact and possibly bring light to someone's bad day. I implemented this new goal of mine while I was in the hospital, without even knowing it. I was positive during my stay because I knew it would help me be okay and recover. My positive attitude left an impact on the staff and they were ultimately upset when I left but happy I had gotten better and could move on.

Maya Angelou once said: *"I've learned that people will forget what you said, people will forget what you did, but people will never forget how you made them feel."*

This quote is how I live my life, or at least how I try to. By being a positive person, always being nice and leaving a lasting impression because I made someone feel good or made their day better.

When I got out of the hospital, things were hard. It was almost as if I had to start my life over. I was in recovery so I had to go to therapy, my medicine was always changing, and I was constantly exhausted.

Dating and making friends was difficult because I never knew when or if it was okay to tell someone about what happened. Often times, I would tell a guy I was dating and he would ghost me, or I would tell a friend and I would scare them. I was around twenty-four at the time, and I was done messing around. I wanted to find my husband. A few months after my boyfriend and I broke up, I started dating another guy. He was great and very sweet, nothing was wrong with him, but I was still hung up on my ex so I let him know that politely and decided to part ways.

Months before I met my now husband, I had been dating a lot. My mom was not happy about it, but I swear I went on over two hundred dates in a year span. As I said before, I was not messing around. I was going to find my husband.

Going on over two hundred dates does not sound great, but I learned a lot about myself and what I wanted in a man. For the longest time, I was super focused on things that truly did not matter. I would give up my morals and change who I was to be with someone who was not right for me. I decided enough was enough, and I took some time to look into what I wanted and decided to make a list of what truly mattered in a life partner. I do not remember the list exactly but I know the first point was they had to be religious; the second was that they had to be the country type because I am country at heart. I determined the last three were not deal breakers but would have been nice, including being musical and having blond or brown hair with blue eyes.

Juggling dating, working, and therapy was hard but I made it all work. I was determined to make a great recovery. I had a few jobs here and there, but because of everything going on, it was hard to keep a job longer than a month or so. This set me back a long time in my professional career; it has been a few years since I left the hospital and I have not gone far in any career.

The job at San Diego State University (SDSU) I ultimately lost, through no fault of my own. The Director changed the duties of the position, and it was more suited to a professor instead of me.

Another position I had after this one was a Customer Service Representative position for a termite inspection company. I stayed at this job a bit longer than at SDSU but I ultimately lost it. I had been going through a rough time at that point where for a bit during the day, I could not physically stay awake. I was living on 5-hour energy drinks and not getting any sleep at night. Almost every day I would struggle to stay awake around nine or eleven in the morning. It was not long before this started becoming an issue and negatively affecting my work. My boss was not very understanding when I informed her of what was going on as best I could. Another issue was that part of my duties included answering the phone. I was still learning, so sometimes I would accidentally hang up on customers who called in. She decided to let me go. I do not blame her. I was still recovering, and it just was not the right job for me.

My next job was working at Domino's as a Delivery Expert. This job was decent, and I was not let go. I am forever grateful I had this job.

I did, however, quit a few months after I started.

In October of 2018, my family received news that my Gram had suffered a hemorrhagic stroke and had to be hospitalized. Since she suffered from a stroke, she was not able to drive for three months. I had not known this information until later when my dad came to me with an idea. He asked me if I would be interested in moving to Texas and helping Gram while she recovered. I had no hesitation and immediately said yes. One year prior to my Gram's accident, she had uprooted her entire life and moved to San Diego in order to help me recover from mine. I believed this was a blessing from God, because I was able to repay my Gram for her kindness.

Living in Texas with Gram was very fun. I was fortunate to not have many bills other than my car payment so I had enough saved to cover my bills while I stayed with her. I was still having a lot of issues with sleep when I moved there so it was good to have that extra time to help get it under control. There would be a specific time during the day I would just pass out. It usually happened between eleven and two. I would drink about half of a 5-hour energy a day there, but I would still only sleep a few hours a night. I would wake up around four or five in the morning and just sit and wait for Gram to get up while watching Friends or Supernatural for a few hours. More often than not it was likely Friends since it is my favorite show ever made. Living with Gram was important in my recovery because I had a lot of fun and I was able to relax. It helped me figure out the issues with my sleep schedule.

We spent a lot of time with Gram's group of girlfriends. I got really close with them and called them all my "girls". Hanging out with Gram and the girls all the time helped me learn how to hold conversations better and become social again. For a while after my psychotic break, I was not talkative and was very anti-social. Gram, my family, and the girls helped me overcome this obstacle and learn to hold conversations and engage with others. The girls and I went to dinner, they came over for dinner, we played games, and we even went on a road trip to a college football game. I never got into football; it was more my sister and dad's thing. Whenever they watched, I either played on my phone or went to another room. But spending time with the girls was worth sitting through anything.

My sister and dad's all-time favorite team was playing, and I ended up living my sister's dream of seeing them. Watching football in the stadium was a lot more exciting than on television, I have to say. Attending the game did not make me start watching at home, but it was still a fun experience.

I was not only blessed to see my Gram when I lived in Texas, but the rest of my extended family lived there as well. I was able to visit my nana, grandad, my aunts, uncles, and cousins. My nana took me to a beautiful garden, we played games, cooked dinner, and had family get-togethers. One of my aunts took me on fun excursions to a play, shopping, and short visits to my other aunt's house together as well. Spending this time with my extended family was not just good for my health, it was good for my soul. I was able to form stronger bonds and get to know my family a bit better.

Thanksgiving was coming, and my mom decided to come visit and join us all for the holiday. Before she arrived, I decided it was time to share the true story with some of my other family members.

We were going to sit down and tell her family together at a family dinner. Prior to this, I had sat down with my Aunt Karen, Gram, and Uncle Malcolm at *Cracker Barrel* and let them know the whole, accurate story. Gram and I went to visit my Uncle Chuck and Royd where I planned to tell them the real story as well. It was still hard for me to talk about the ordeal at this point, so Gram helped me tell them while we all drove in the car to dinner. Through sharing my story, I learned new things about my family. Apparently, my nana had what seemed to be a mental break as well in her early years of motherhood. I came to learn mental illness runs in my family, and that is not bad; just points toward the fact I need to continue to be vigilant in my care and recovery. Sharing my story has aided in my recovery.

When I told my story to a group of youth at my church in San Diego, it was therapeutic for me. I realized that day how helpful my story would be to others, whenever I was ready to share it. My story helped change one of the young girls' lives because her mother was also in psychosis. She told some of her story and said it was the first time she had talked about it with anyone else.

After a few short months with my family, I headed back to San Diego. I assumed things were going to start getting better when I returned but my recovery was a long process.

The story I told to the youth is found below:

My Story (as written at the time):

My name is Erin Wall, and I have been attending Hope United Methodist Church since I was 10, and I was in youth here like all of you.

I'm now 25 years old and married..... I wanted to share my story with you and your parents because I think it's important to help others.

Have you ever wanted something so bad that you were unknowingly destroying your life to get it?

Well, that was me over 3 years ago. I was dating a guy (we had been dating for about 2 years in 2017) that I would have done anything for, and that mindset helped me make bad choices. My relationship with my boyfriend was crazy – we would break up and get back together multiple times, and he also liked to keep me away from my family sometimes. Nothing mattered to me but being with him. I was graduating college in

May of 2017, and he was getting out of the Marines and moving back to Wisconsin. I wanted us to get married, but he said he would not marry me unless I made a lot of money.

This was the catalyst for me deciding to apply to Officer Candidate School for the Navy because I knew I could make enough money as a Naval Officer to make my boyfriend happy. It was a really hard process, but I made it through and was selected. He supported my efforts, but when I made it, he was also surprised. I now know looking back he never thought I would make it. He didn't have confidence in me or really love me. He was just manipulating me.

When he left to go back home after getting out of the Marines, he wanted to take a break, and I kept trying to convince him that was not a good idea. I even went to see him for a week, but he worked all week and I stayed in the hotel room all by myself, getting depressed. My parents were even worried about me,

but I was hiding how I was really feeling.

When I came back, we broke up. Even though I had applied for Officer Candidate School (OCS) for my boyfriend, I decided it would still be a good thing for me to attend and *attempt to get my life on track for myself, instead of him. Right before I left for OCS, he called me and said he wanted to get back together. I was so excited to go visit him.*

My parents had concerns, but I just explained them all away because this was exactly what I thought I wanted. During that trip, I made some really bad decisions to impress my boyfriend. He suggested we do some drugs and not just things like smoking weed. He wanted me to take some LSD and ecstasy, so I took them, trying to impress him. He had gotten into these drugs and told me that everything would be okay, but it wasn't. I had a really horrible experience. It was very traumatic and a lot of scary images and thoughts lasted for over 12 hours.

When I got back home, I didn't tell my parents, but I did let it slip that my boyfriend was into doing drugs. My mom was concerned and asked me if I had done any drugs while visiting him, but I lied to her. The next day, I left for OCS.

While at OCS, I started having irrational and paranoid thoughts. I was freaking out, not eating, not showering, and the constant yelling was making my brain crazy. They put me on suicide watch because I was telling my roommates I wanted to commit suicide. Somehow, in spite of my brain not functioning properly, I found the courage and momentary sanity to DOR, which is Drop on Request from OCS.

This means they have to let you go. I texted my parents and immediately they knew something was wrong with me from the very first few texts.

We later realized I was in a mental state called psychosis. Psychosis is an alternate reality. Everyone who has psychosis experiences a different alternate reality. Mine was filled with terrifying visions of people hurting me and my family, paranoia about being arrested by the FBI, my dad losing his job, and people coming to get me. I also thought food wasn't really food. I couldn't fully function and was afraid to be left alone. I would also freeze in certain positions, or walk around non-stop with a lot of energy. I also thought about suicide when I got home from OCS.

We went to a therapist, and she told my mom she thought I was having some psychosis or PTSD symptoms.

She encouraged my mom to get me in to see a psychiatrist, but this therapist wasn't very helpful.

She also told my mom therapy wouldn't help, only medicine. Over the course of the next couple of weeks, I went to see the therapist again while waiting to be seen by the psychiatrist, but nothing changed.

My boyfriend decided to come visit, and my parents were okay with that because he was the only one who could seem to get any kind of emotion out of me. Once he arrived, he told my parents he didn't think anything was wrong with me, although everything was wrong with me. My brain wasn't working properly.

One night, I told my family I wanted to embrace what was in my brain, and all of us, being unaware what was fully happening inside my brain, thought that was a good thing, but what it meant was I went into a crazy psychotic state. I was talking and moving non-stop. My parents decided the best thing for me was to go to the hospital because they didn't know what else to do. We started at an ER, and Pastor Brian met us there to help my family and just be there with them. From there, I was transferred the next day to an inpatient facility.

I stayed at an inpatient facility for three weeks. It wasn't easy for me or my parents. I came home for about a week, and

121

had a relapse because my medicine was lowered too quickly by the hospital doctors. I was back in the hospital for about 10 days and came home on Halloween night. 2017. That was the last time I was in the hospital.

The hospital staff helped my parents find a specialized program for people just like me – ages 12-35 and who've had psychosis. At first, I was going several times a week – meeting with my therapist, my psychiatrist, and group therapy. I didn't always like it, and didn't want to go. My parents required me to go – which did make me mad at first, but I now realize it was the best thing. My grandma also moved in with us for 3 months to help me because I couldn't drive and was scared to be left alone. She was a big help to my family.

I now have an official diagnosis which is Bipolar. When I was younger, I was incorrectly diagnosed with ADHD. Which can often mimic Bipolar. My new doctor took over a year to diagnose me – she's very thorough like that. If left untreated, Bipolar can result in psychosis, like it did for me. Diagnosis also has to do with recovery, and my recovery is what they consider to be a full recovery.

Both my doctors also think my illicit drug use helped trigger my psychotic episode because it put me into a manic state, and I had also swung out of a depression from being broken up with by my boyfriend.

After this experience, I realized how important my faith has been in God, and my church family. It helped me and my parents during all this hard time. My recovery has also been remarkable according to my doctors but also I think doable for anyone if you can get help and decide you want a better life – it takes A LOT of work, all the time. I go to all my appointments, take my medicine, and practice self-care. I make sure to monitor if something is off with me or not, and I always tell my husband and family.

Now I'm working full time at a wonderful company, and I'm back in school to get my MBA. I also met a young man who I feel God placed in my life to be my partner in life forever. We got married in August of 2019. I told him all about my crazy experience and none of it scared him or made him not want to be with me. I told my mom I had to be honest about all of it since it's a part of who I am.

The story I hope to share is - don't be in toxic relationships – if a relationship keeps you away from friends and family, it's not healthy. Don't hide things from your family or friends, and don't do drugs. I know the saying "don't do drugs" is one you hear often, but you never know how it will affect your brain negatively, and once you find out, it's too late.

Last but not least, make sure to ask for help when you need it, because I asked for help and it saved my life. Do not think people are going to judge you, because the people who love you will not.

I found the story a few months ago. It was typed out on a few pieces of paper. I quickly realized how much of the writing does not sound like me.

I wanted to marry Shim, very badly, but that want did not destroy my life. Going through psychosis seemed to have saved me. And I know how odd that sounds, but I never found out who I truly was, or began to, until a few years after my recovery.

Furthermore, Shim never kept me from my family; every time I stayed with him it was because I wanted to. Living at home was not bad, but when I stayed with Shim, I had a different kind of freedom I did not experience at home with my parents. I was able to go places and not be required to tell him where I was going or when I would be home. Often times, I would because I wanted to, but I was never at risk of getting in trouble if I forgot to.

Shim said he did not want to get married unless I made a lot of money, and that is fine, because he was honest. I have no harsh feelings toward him at all. I wanted to change him and make him want to marry me throughout our entire relationship, and that was not fair to either of us.

I never took LSD to impress Shim. I decided to do it on my own. He never pressured me into anything. It was our idea for me to join the Navy, but that was never the sole reason. I was going to go to OCS whether Shim and I were together or not. I wanted to join the Navy to make a better life for myself, whether he was in it or not.

After I dropped out of OCS, he did not take things well when he came to visit. Not a lot of people understand psychosis; my own family barely understood it before I was in it. From what I can remember and what I gathered from our messages, he handled the experience as best as he could. I do not know how I would react in a situation like that one. I presume he handled it as best as he could.

Shim and I had an interesting relationship. We were so different, but, somehow, we just worked. However, we were not meant to be. After he left to go back to Wisconsin, we slowly grew apart. I do not remember how things between us finally ended but I know it was on good terms. Him and I talk every now and then, which is good because I dislike burning bridges.

CHAPTER TEN

My Saving Grace

March 2019

My husband and I started officially dating on March 3rd of 2019, eight days before I started my new job at General Atomics. I do not know the exact day we met, but our love story is truly like none other.

Jake and I met on a dating app similar to Tinder called Bumble. There is a big difference between Bumble and Tinder. Bumble is designed to give women the power. Which means men will only match if a woman swipes right on them and they can only chat if the woman initiates the conversation. The CEO of Bumble was on the creative team of Tinder, she even named it, but after she was sexually harassed and pushed off the team, she created Bumble.

I distinctly remember seeing my husband's profile. He looked kind of young and maybe a bit nerdy. He did not have the best photos, so I was not able to tell how cute he was, but for some reason, I knew something was there. After a few minutes of going through his profile, I swiped right and went off to bed. The main information I received from his profile was that he was a Marine and stationed on Camp Pendleton, CA. He was definitely up the alley way of the guys I usually dated.

The next morning, I woke up to realize we had matched. We talked for a few minutes and I swear his second message was telling me he was from North Carolina. I have always wanted to marry someone from Texas or North Carolina. Super opposite states, I know, but I am weird. So, my second message to this complete stranger was that I wanted to marry him.

We had only been talking maybe five minutes. At this point in my life, I had been dating a lot and I no longer wanted to play games and was always trying to be upfront and honest with the guys I potentially dated. Maybe I was testing him, I do not know exactly why I said that, but he responded perfectly and we chose to hang out that day.

I still had my military ID from when my dad was serving in the Navy, so I drove to hang out with him on base and we watched *Brooklyn Nine-Nine*. I had been talking to a few other guys at the time right before I met Jake, and one of them texted me while I was with him, so I spent some time messaging him while watching TV with Jake. That was not the best decision on my end, because Jake broke it off, but I do not regret it. Jake and I ended up getting together in the end and that is all that matters … not without some roadblocks, however.

The guy I was messaging with on the base ended up ghosting me in the end, so that took care of itself, but there was one more possible issue.

I had met another guy that was great. He had a great job, he treated me very well, went out of his way to see me, and was just great all around. The other guy lived pretty far away, almost two hours.

But the thought of Jake and what I did, I could not shake. I ended up reaching out to Jake to see if we might be able to give it another shot, maybe go on an actual date, instead of hanging out in his room. He was nice but I knew he must not have been happy with me. I just recently found out he told his friend Joey about me asking for a second chance and Joey said to give it a shot, because what did he have to lose? If Joey had been in a bad mood or something happened, which might have made him say no, that Jake would have turned me down and we would have never gone out again.

I had still gone out to dinner with the other guy while I waited for Jake's response.

His name was Steven. Like I said, he was great but I was not completely invested. Steven took me to *Sea World* for our second date. It was great. I had tons of fun; we rode roller coasters over thirty times. During the day at Sea World, I checked in with Jake from time to time, and we planned to have our second date later that night. I was honest with Steven about Jake, and vice-versa. I told them both I would have an answer as to who I wanted to exclusively date by the end of the weekend, because I was a little torn. I was pretty certain I was going to pick Jake but I could not predict the future, so I told Steven I would let him know. After our day at Sea World ended, Steven took me back home and I got ready for my date with Jake.

Jake's friends were headed down to San Diego that night, so he hitched a ride with them and met me at a movie theater. We saw *How to Train Your Dragon 3* at the movie theater. We talked, laughed, held hands, and just had an amazing time. I recently told Jake that *DreamWorks* should be the sponsor of our lives because watching that movie was the beginning of our love story.

After the movie, his friends were not ready to come back and pick him up so we decided to hang out in my car for a bit until they were ready. We talked for hours about anything and everything. It was like we had known each other forever. I knew then he was the right man for me. I swear we both fell in love that night; we were just too afraid to say it. The next day, I told Steven my decision, and Jake and I officially started dating.

Our next date was that very same day. Since his friends still weren't ready, he went to church with my parents and me. After church, we went to lunch at this restaurant called Chicken Charlie's where he asked my parents permission to date me. And that was the beginning of our crazy love story.

A lot happened in a few short months. I started a new job, I met the love of my life, and my recovery was continuing to progress nicely with therapy and my medication.

When I left the hospital for the second time, my mom received a recommendation on where I should go to continue my recovery. She was recommended the UCSD Care program in San Diego. This mental health facility was among the top-rated facility in the nation for young adults with psychosis. This was the best place to send me for the time being, and my psychiatrist and psychologist were essential to my improvement. I always loved my psychiatrist, Dr. D, but it took me awhile to warm up to my psychologist, Dr. M. My Gram told me she thinks it took me awhile to warm up to Dr. M because she tried to get me to open up and talk. I started seeing them very shortly after I broke out of psychosis, and for a while, I did not want to talk at all, but, eventually, I started opening up and, later on, I loved Dr. M.

My start date at GA was not until March, but before then, I spent some time working on myself and having laid back jobs. While I was not working, I would attend this weekly group meeting at the Care program. I think going to this group helped me open up. The other young adults in this group did not talk much, which pushed me to open up more. After I started at GA, I would only see Dr. M every two weeks, sometimes every three depending on what was going on. I was reserved for a while because I was not ready to talk about what happened, because it made me uncomfortable. But after a bit, I realized she was there for me to talk to about anything, not just psychosis. At one point, she told she was Armenian and that made me happy because my best friend was Armenian as well. Many people do not like their therapists right away, and I was one of those, but now I have learned to give it time and find a way to relate to your therapist and then the relationship will develop.

Things seemed to have been going great. I had been enjoying my job, I was dating an amazing guy, but Jake had been keeping something from me. Apparently, he had been set to deploy near the end of the year and was afraid to tell me. That did not scare me, since I had already been through a deployment with my ex.

Jake and I wasted no time falling in love and moving forward. We said I love you after dating for about a week. A few days later, I concocted a plan. We were already in love, we knew we wanted to spend our lives together, so why not get married? Much to my surprise, Jake agreed with my proposal.

Less than two weeks into our relationship, we started planning our marriage. We were crazy, but excited. We planned the perfect day, and took it from there. I started researching my dream engagement ring and sent Jake a screenshot when I found it.

Jake lived on the Marine Corps base Camp Pendleton, over an hour away. Since he lived far away, we were only able to see one another on the weekends. Every weekend until we got married, I would drive to base and pick Jake up, we would spend the weekend together, and I would drive him back on Sundays. Only seeing each other on the weekends was a little hard on our new relationship but we made it work. There were a few times I saw him during the week, but over a span of five months, it was only a max of three times.

Our second weekend together, Jake bought me a promise ring from Walmart. It was beautiful, and the first out of multiple rings I received.

Every weekend together was fun. We would go on adventures, such as going to the San Diego Zoo, taking a drive to sunset cliffs and carving our names into one of the cliffs, and going to *Sea World* with my family. We even went to church almost every weekend.

We would text and talk every day during the week and chat about what we would do the next weekend we saw each other. We grew extremely close in a very short amount of time, and fell head over heels in love with one another.

On May 31st 2019, Jake's favorite country music artist, *Justin Moore*, was performing at the Del Mar fairgrounds, so I decided to surprise him with tickets. I did not know that his best friend was also going, so he found out his surprise before we arrived there. We had ordered my engagement ring a few weeks before then and we went to pick it up prior to the concert. I was not allowed to see my wedding ring, but I had picked it out and had an idea of what it looked like.

I had no idea that Jake had a surprise planned for me, too. We had a great time at the concert. Jake sang along to every song and recorded almost everything until he ran out of space on his phone. His friend and him had been being pretty secretive the whole night and going off alone to talk and leaving me alone with his friend's girlfriend, which I did not like. I can be awkward when left alone with people I do not know. When we got back to the car, his friend and him were playing *Justin Moore*, and I was talking to his friend's girlfriend. She asked me how Jake and I met. Unbeknownst to me, Jake's friend told her to start recording because a romantic song came on. I was telling her how Jake and I met, and that I told him I wanted to marry him right away, and how we deleted our Bumbles and I no longer had the messages. As I said those words, Jake got down on one knee behind me. I turned around and was utterly shocked and unable to speak. He asked me to marry him, and, of course, I said yes. In the words of Chandler Bing, we were a "betrothed couple".

Two crazy kids were engaged, and in July, we were blessed to be able to visit some of my extended family in Texas. One of my Gram's friends offered to throw us a wedding shower, and I agreed because I wanted Jake to meet the rest of the family.

Around the same time, Jake had flown home to say goodbye to his grandpa, who was suffering from cancer and had passed away. I flew off to Texas separate for a few days, and Jake met me there a few days later. We stayed with my Gram and went to the shower. Jake was able to meet my uncles, aunts, Gram's friends, and almost all of my other grandparents. It was a wonderful time … and something very special to be able to do together before Jake left for deployment a few months later.

The next month, we were planning to get married. I chose August 3rd as our day, because it was six months after we started officially dating. Right before the wedding, I realized it was really five, but that did not derail our plans. The military sure tried to mess it up, as it seems the military tries to mess up everything.

Jake was sent to the field for training about a week before our wedding. Despite the fact he had been telling his command for over a month to make sure he was free the weekend of August 3rd.

My mom had a big surprise planned for us. She did not keep me in the loop at first because she thought I would spill the secret. She ended up telling me after a bit of pushing that she was flying Jake's parents in for our wedding, and she was getting worried because she was afraid Jake was not going to make it. I did not know either. Jake was able to come back the day before our wedding, thankfully, and my dad, his parents, and I went to pick him up from base and bring him back to our house. When we arrived on base, I went upstairs to help Jake finish packing for the weekend, and my dad got his parents situated for the surprise downstairs. When we walked downstairs, Jake noticed his parents almost immediately and was extremely surprised. He embraced his mom and started crying. Jake and I will always cherish that gift from my parents. I had not met any of his family before we got engaged, which made meeting his parents the day before our wedding more special.

We exchanged our vows at my childhood church, and my favorite Pastor officiated our service. Since our first wedding was rushed, it was a small ceremony and we only had around fifty guests. My family was there along with a lot of friends, church family, Jake's parents, and my gram. My mom also surprised me with a professional photographer for the event.

The ceremony went perfect. We exchanged our vows and were a married couple. We were unable to have many of the wedding traditions; no first dance or daddy daughter dance. We had time for food afterward, and a bit of fellowship with family and friends. My mom made tacos and they were great, and we also had cake. I was obsessed with Costco cake and Jake loved red velvet, so my parents bought a Costco cake and made a red velvet cake for Jake.

Our wedding day went great and we were elated. My parents blessed us with a minimoon at a local hotel where I used to work called Rancho Bernardo Inn. A few hours after the wedding, we left to our hotel and spent the night just relaxing. We were given complimentary chocolate covered strawberries and champagne. We spent some time in the hot tub, relaxed in comfortable robes, took a bubble bath, and watched movies. At some point in the night, we had dinner, too, but I do not recall where. I think we ordered pizza and wings. We stayed up and hung out in bliss as long as we could until we drifted off to sleep.

While we were waiting for Jake to move in, Jake was at work one day and he was sweeping and he bent down. When he stood up, he hit his head on a breaker box and cut his head open. He called me and let me know what was going on, and I left to go get him to bring him to our house for the weekend. When I got to him, he did not want to go to the hospital, but I knew he was in pain and decided to take him there anyway. They diagnosed him with a concussion and said he should rest and not go back to work right away.

I was upset because he had to spend a week in darkness in his barracks room alone instead of at our house. Jake had not talked to me for a week and I assumed he had gone to the field as they were supposed to. His friend told me he had talked to Jake, so he was not in the field, so I wasn't sure why he hadn't talked to me. We ended up having one of our first big fights, unfortunately, because he has bad communication issues, but we got through it.

Shortly after that, Jake finally moved in. We cleaned out his room, loaded up both cars, and moved into my room together. It was a little crowded but we made it work for a few months until he deployed. We agreed since he was leaving, it would be best if I was not alone. We paid my parents rent, which allowed us to save money as well.

A few months into my marriage, my family was planning on going on a cruise to celebrate my parents' wedding anniversary. This was the same week Jake was set to deploy and we were afraid I was not going to be home before he left to say goodbye.

Our cruise was November 11th to the 16th of 2019, and Jake was preparing to leave on the 18th. Since Jake was leaving, I decided to go back to school, and I was set to begin while on our cruise. But doing schoolwork on the cruise became an issue quickly. I decided to focus on excursions and family time during the day, and would sometimes skip family dinners to finish up my homework at night. Vartouhy, my best friend of fifteen years, and I hung out in the room and ordered room service instead of meeting everyone else for dinner a few nights during the cruise, and this did not please my mother. Vartouhy was surprised with how negatively my family treated me and let me know.

Sad to say, this cruise was the start of a long, miserable battle I fought with my family, which I will talk more about later.

When we returned home, Jake and I had two days together before he left. I do not remember us ever leaving my room other than to eat or use the restroom. We stayed in bed to watch movies and cuddle. I showed him a new animated movie he had not seen yet, and he loved it.

The night before Jake left, we had a good cry and a long embrace. Before we went to sleep, we promised each other we would make it work, no matter what.

I could sit here and say deployment was easy, but I'd be lying. Our love was strong enough to make it work, and, in the end, we got through it, but going through that deployment was the hardest thing we ever experienced. Jake and I had known each other less than a year, and he left for over six months. The first year of marriage is often hard for any newlyweds, but Jake and I had it a lot tougher. We got married, but we moved in with my parents and did not have our own space. Two months after marriage, we were separated for over half a year, which can cause a lot of strain. While Jake was deployed, we had our fair share of fights. In fact, we almost ended our marriage throughout his deployment, multiple times. Luckily for us, God, our family, friends, and our love were all on our side and we made it through the deployment.

One of the great things about Jake and me is that even though we have differences, we share one important thing.

Determination. Jake and I both understand marriage is not perfect and requires hard work and resilience at times to ensure the relationship stays strong.

Jake's deployment was hard, not only because of the time difference but we were both on edge and being apart was hard. The Covid-19 pandemic hit shortly after he left, which made his deployment get extended by a month.

Jake had his stress to deal with, and I was dealing with my own strain at home.

CHAPTER ELEVEN

A New Job and Journey

A few months before I met Jake, I received an interview at the company my dad works at, General Atomics (GA). My dad helped me get a chance to interview. I performed pretty well, and after a few months of waiting, I received news I was offered the position. During the time of waiting, I was offered a position to sell life insurance, but, ultimately, I decided to accept the position at GA.

I did not know what to expect with this new position, but I was very excited to begin this new journey. It was not long before I got bored with the job and no longer wanted to be there. My days consisted of burning CDs on one computer, scanning them on another, and then transferring the data on the CD to another computer. I was told the position was never meant for someone to stay in for an extended period of time; they knew no one would be happy there long-term. I started school to help with my boredom, and because GA reimbursed me for my classes, it helped a bit but not tremendously, so I started an independent rescue to save cats and kittens in the greater San Diego area, which I will expand on later.

I worked at GA through the pandemic. I never enjoyed my job, but once the pandemic hit, it just got worse. I was alone all day and extremely lonely. I started to develop severe depression. The one friend I made was able to work from home during the pandemic and I was still in the office, so we could not go to lunch together anymore.

Not many people in my life understood why I disliked my job. I did not try to explain because I felt my reasonings would not be understood. I always perceived my job was meant for a high-schooler. It was beyond simple and mundane.

My favorite days were Thursday because I had another task to do, which was a lot more involved and fun. But every other day was boring.

My department was known for being toxic, unbeknownst to me. Our HR representative was extremely unprofessional in my opinion and did not take any complaints seriously.

I was in this position for about a year until it was just too much to handle. One night after an amazing day working with my rescue (which I will talk more about later), I just snapped. Out of nowhere, my head filled with intense pressure and nothing I did helped. I started crying and could not breathe very well. My husband rushed me to the hospital, and by the time we got there, I had calmed down a bit and they could not do much for me. The Doctor suggested I get a new job, and I told them I was trying. I was released and my husband took me home.

The night after the hospital was dreadful. I spent the entire night awake and crying because I knew I had to go back to work the next day.

When I went to work the next day, I was not there long, and my boss did not think I was going to come in either. We talked for a bit and I told her I wanted to talk to our new manager about different options. She told me there were not any other options, and my chest began to tighten. I felt I could not breathe and my eyes filled with tears. I did not know what to do. I was afraid to tell her how upset I was, so I reached out to one of the security guards I knew, Aaron. He called the paramedics to come check on me, and they decided I should go to the hospital. I had the choice of them taking me or my boss; my boss took me. The car ride to the hospital was sort of awkward, but I am thankful she drove me.

This trip to the hospital was similar to the last one. By the time I arrived, I was calmed down and the Doctor again suggested I should get another job. I took this second suggestion seriously and began medical leave the next day. I was able to take some time and focus on self-care. I searched for other jobs, worked on my rescue, and hung out with friends.

I was on leave for around a month and doing pretty well. After the month was over, my psychiatrist said she was unable to extend my medical leave. I called and quit my job the next day. A few days later, I received a call for my exit interview. I was blind-sided and in line for security at the airport with Jake. He had just returned from deployment and we were on our way to visit his family for Thanksgiving. I voiced my concerns to her in the best way possible, but she blatantly ignored all my concerns. Since the day I quit GA, I have told myself I will never stay in a position again that compromises my mental health. I decided on that day to always put my mental health first, no matter the circumstance. There will always be another job, but I only have one mind.

CHAPTER TWELVE

Pandemic Predicament

November 2019

Shortly after Jake left, the Covid-19 pandemic hit and it came like a freight train. It was hard to make friends in general, but the pandemic seemed to make it worse. Throughout Jake's entire deployment, I attempted to make friends, time and time again, but it continuously failed.

My mom told me as a military spouse, I would make the best friends to ever have. Sadly, that was far from the truth. I remember one time I was messaging with a spouse whose husband was deployed with mine. I thought we could be good friends because we were going through the same exact thing. We made plans to meet at an event later that night. I let her know my mom and I planned to head up after I got off work and we would meet her there. Later, she messaged me saying her and her friend were going to go and they would meet us. When my mom and I left my work, I told her we were on our way. About half an hour later, I received a message from her that her and the friend were leaving, because they felt awkward and out of place. I told her multiple times we were almost there and if they could just wait a bit that would be nice. They left, and my mom and I continued on. It was an okay night. I was upset, but at least we received a free dinner.

Making friends was really hard, as you can tell. I would experience drama every single day, and it became very heavy on my heart. I would have mental breakdowns often. I remember driving home from church one day, and I was dealing with more drama from a spouse. I started screaming and crying while I was driving and had to try and pull myself together so I would make it home safe. I made it home safe, but I still have a lot of emotional scarring from being a military spouse I need to work through. I would often tell my mom what I was going through, and I did not believe my concerns were ever truly heard … until one night.

I was going through a lot and wanted a friend so badly. At that point, I was only seeing my best friend once a week or less and I was desperate for any sort of relationship outside of home. I reached out to another spouse for friendship and it blew up in my face yet again. My meltdown was almost instantaneous. At the time, I was getting dressed, so I ended up running around my room half dressed, screaming and crying at my mom to finally be heard. Some of the things I said included: *These women are crazy, these women are evil, these women are devils. I have tried and tried and tried to make friends but I do not have any. I am not the problem anymore.*

After that night, I stopped trying to make friends. I do regret this decision, but I decided to be a lurker on the Facebook groups instead. That was not the best decision on my part, but it was the better decision for my mental health at the time.

I survived the rest of Jake's deployment by acting similar to every other spouse I interacted with; by being a bitch.

One specific incident occurred around the time Kobe Bryant died, which I believe was the same night of the meltdown with my mom. I have nothing against the man, and I am sorry for his family's loss, but I had posted multiple posts on my personal page about how the military never gets recognition when thousands of families lose loved ones every day, but if a famous person dies, it is as if the whole world is over and I believed it was wrong. I had forgotten that one of the spouses I had problems with prior was my friend, and she decided to comment on my posts multiple times, arguing with me. This did not sit right with me and I snapped. I do regret what I said but I was coming off of five or so months of turmoil so give me a break. Under one of her comments, I replied something similar to:

Ya know I bet you would probably be one of those girls who moves on right away when their husband dies and I feel bad for your husband.

A lot of my personal friends started attacking me for what I said, and I deleted the post shortly after. She decided to tell my mom on me later, which is typical "high school" military spouse behavior.

Jake was deployed for seven months, and throughout the entire seven months, I did not make one friend who stuck around.

However, I found a pen pal from Florida. We talked often, but have not met yet, which is unfortunate. I eventually made a friend, and she is amazing, but we did not meet until a bit after Jake returned from deployment.

My parents helped a lot with mine and Jake's relationship during his deployment. I will always be thankful for that, but our relationship was not the best at times.

A few months into Jake's deployment, I reconnected with an old friend. I think I posted on my SnapChat story about being depressed about something, probably military spouse drama, and he asked if I was okay. Our friendship blossomed from there. We started talking every day, about anything and everything. We would quiz each other on random things because we were both in school, or complain about how much our lives sucked. Either way, I was elated to finally have someone to talk to. My newfound friendship did not sit right with my mother. Jake did not care; we have always been open and honest, and he knew I was talking to this guy every day and what we would talk about. At this time, I was still on my parents' cell phone plan and not technically paying for the service. This made my mother think she could know who I was talking to 24/7 and why I was talking to them. Which I do and do not understand. I was paying rent, so I deserved to be treated as an adult and have freedom as well as my own private matters.

Either way, I am a people pleaser so I let my mom know about my friend once and I thought that was it. Almost every time I was texting on my phone, she would continuously ask who I was talking to, and every time I said it was my male friend, it would be an issue. One day, the situation was regrettably escalated.

I remember sitting at the kitchen table, minding my own business, writing a paper and messaging my friend. She was in the kitchen and asked me who I was talking to. I knew she did not like me talking to him, so I lied and said it was someone else. I am not a good liar so she knew it was him in the end. A few minutes later, she escalated the situation and accused me of cheating on Jake with this man. Understandably, I became angry and lashed out at her, because accusing me of that was uncalled for. Then the yelling and screaming began and my dad became involved. I remember him coming in and yelling, then throwing me outside until I calmed down. Sad to say, I still have a lot of built-up trauma from this situation. Healing will take a while because I never received an apology from what my mother said. I do forgive them, because that will aid in my personal healing and I try not to hold onto grudges.

I was let inside a few minutes later after being coerced into an apology I should not have had to make, and I got dressed to leave. Since Covid was so prevalent at that time, the one friend I had made I had not seen in months. Thank heavens, she let me come over that day for a bit to cool off from the situation.

Making friends was hard, but having adult freedom was almost impossible. One time, I had a bag packed and was going to a boudoir shoot to surprise Jake with some photos. My mom saw my bag and asked where I was going. As I said, I am not a good liar and I told her the truth after many minutes of her persistence. Covid had just started so she was not sure the space was clean and I would not bring home any diseases. Her response was that I could leave but I would not be able to come home and would have to find somewhere else to stay for two weeks if I chose to go take the photos. My mother did not see this as controlling even though it was an ultimatum. Despite the fact I was paying rent and received my mail there, so, legally, it was my home, too. I ultimately chose not to go because I did not have the money or friends to stay anywhere else.

155

Looking back now, I suppose my mother was just concerned because my dad had been going through a lot of health issues and she did not want to risk him getting sick. The entire situation could have been handled better on both of our ends. Luckily, we have moved past this and our relationship is much better.

Funnily enough, about a month or so later, my mother was starting to get fed up with the regulations and then it was okay for me to go. This was infuriating. I was an adult, I was paying rent, I should have been able to go in the first place. I understand their point of view. Yes, I was putting myself and them at a potential risk, but I was twenty-five-years-old and the photographer and I were grown up enough to take the necessary precautions. If she was unable to conduct her business in a safe manner, then she would not still be in business in San Diego.

My mother is a very clean person and that is fine, but she used to push her ideologies onto me and I did not enjoy it. I am a clean person, I try to keep my house clean, but with eleven animals, it is hard at times and I often choose my mental health over a spotless house. My animals are healthy and so are we which makes the house not being perfectly clean fine. It has been hard for me to get past the mental block of thinking a dirty house is bad or means you're lesser than. I am trying to learn the balance between a healthy mind and a clean house.

Our differences in cleanliness was always an argument between my mother and me. I know she was trying to help but it caused more damage than good. I would leave one thing in the sink and almost every single time would get a text in the group chat with my dad reading something like, **Who left this in the sink**?, and then would proceed to get a lecture on cleanliness. Our relationship became so torn she once told me she would rather pay for me to live in the hospital than with them because it would be cheaper. That statement was very traumatic for me because it was highly untrue. I would constantly pay for my own food, I was rarely home, and Jake and I paid some rent. It has taken some time to get past that comment, and I work toward moving past everything every day because I do want a better relationship, but it is hard sometimes. It is difficult to understand how someone who dropped everything and left in one day to come and save me could say those words. But she did, and I am working toward healing from the wounds they caused.

Every day I went to work, I spent half a day continuously depressed over everything. I am extremely surprised I did not have a mental breakdown every single day. I had my fair share, but it was not every day.

I tried to move out multiple times but it never worked out. Jake convinced me to stay and push through it, and I had no one to help me move. Luckily, I made it through Jake's deployment living at home, and everything was a bit better when Jake returned. My relationship with my family became worse, but we eventually overcame our differences.

CHAPTER THIRTEEN

Moving Out and Moving Up

June 2020

A month or two before Jake was set to come home, I started a new adventure; buying our first home. The experience was pretty crazy to deal with on my own, but I had a lot of time on my hands, and my parents helped. We had a lot of options – buy a condominium, purchase land and buy a modular home, or try and find a small house. But we had to make sure; we were in between both of our jobs, which limited our options. Ultimately, we decided on purchasing a condominium and my search began. I picked some options, and my dad and I went to look at them one day. I liked a lot of them but none of them stood out to me.

A few days went by, during which this one cute, affordable place kept making its way back to me. I asked our realtor if it accepted VA loans because not all do and she said no, but I did some digging. We found out it did and the next day, my dad and I were off to see the new option. I walked in and, within seconds, I knew this was the perfect place for our new home. I had to convince Jake, because he was not too keen on me buying a place without him seeing it first. Later on the same day our offer was put in, I received a call and the condominium was ours. We had our first home to move into together when he arrived home a few weeks later. I was elated and Jake was excited.

A few weeks later, we found out the person we bought our house from worked for the company I worked for and was moving. It was a sign from God, and we were ready to start our lives together in our new home.

Jake's homecoming was different, but I still tried to make it very special.

I decorated my parents' house for his return, and a photographer took photos of us in front of our house the next day after some much-needed rest.

I made a cheese-themed welcome home sign. The sign I made read, "Jacob Greene, I'm Cheesin, You're my baby, We bout to go crazy, Come kiss your lady". I based the rest of his homecoming on this sign. Everything was cheese-themed. There was yellow streamers, gold and yellow balloons, poppers hanging from the ceiling, I made a cheese plate, and bought a cheesecake. I was going to wear a cheese hat, but I was not able to find a cheap one before he was set to come home. Instead, I opted to wear cute yellow boppers. I was so wrapped up in him finally being home that I forgot to wear them for our professional photos. We do not have any professional photos with me and my boppers on but we got one selfie together on my phone. His homecoming was cheese themed because I sent him cheesy poems all the time throughout his entire deployment. Homecoming was perfect, and we spent the next few days getting reacquainted before starting to pack and move into our first home.

Moving is potentially stressful, but we made it through with the help of each other, my family, and some friends. Jake and I packed up our whole room, but my dad and a friend helped us load everything onto the truck, trailer, and into my car. Then my dad, sister, and her husband helped us unload at the house. All in all, it was a team effort, and Jake and I were so glad to finally be moved in together and start our somewhat normal marriage.

One of the first things Jake and I did was foster a kitten. Someone I knew from church had a friend who bought a kitten in San Diego and was unable to pick her up right away, so she needed someone to keep her until she was able to. She named her Dinah Rhea; Jake and I preferred to call her Rhea. We had so much fun watching Rhea, we decided to get our own kitten shortly after. I joined a lot of Facebook groups to see what kittens may have been available, and one of the very first ones had a foster in it with a female tortoiseshell named Kenzie. She immediately stood out to me, and when I showed her to Jake, he said she was so ugly she was cute. We had our hearts set on Kenzie, and I filled out an application to adopt one of their kittens. We got a time set up to go to their facility and meet the kittens for adoption. One other kitten stood out to me, but I ultimately chose Kenzie. We paid the adoption fee and took her home that day and started thinking of her new name. I thought about calling her Elsa and had a few other choices, but Jake suggested Nala and that just stuck and was her name from that day forward. We had a wonderful few days with Nala and Rhea, but then things took a drastic turn.

Nala started acting weird. She was not eating and she was sleeping a lot. Jake did not think anything of it, but what I like to believe was mother's intuition was nagging at me. Nala was resting on Jake one night, and never woke up for about five hours. We went to sleep, hoping she would get better overnight. The next morning, I woke up and I could not find her, and told Jake to check on her when he woke up. He found her sleeping in one of the drawers connected to our bed frame. I was concerned at that point and told Jake I was going to research and find a vet to take her to. We were both at work by that point and I was unable to go home and pick her up. I was very concerned, so I reached out to my neighbor to see if he could check on her. We had a code on our door to go in instead of a key so he went inside to check and she was still sleeping in my drawer. I was extremely worried, so I asked if he could bring her to me and he agreed. By that time, I had a vet picked out to take her to and I took a longer lunch to check her in and drop her off. Covid was still rampant at this time so they came out to my car, picked her up, and took her into the hospital. I did not see her again for over two days. She had a bad fever and it would not break. They tested her for many diseases, around fifteen, and everything came back negative. She was on an IV the entire time and pumped with fluids. They did a lot of things to try and heal her I did not agree with, so I took her out after she had been in the hospital around 50 hours. She was not 100% better, but a lot of times the stress of a hospital for animals keeps them from getting better. I thought she would get better at home, so I pulled her out. When she came home, it was still a long road to recovery. She was still showing signs of not being well for a few days so I took her to another vet that was open 24 hours and had emergency hours. She was healthy enough to be treated as outpatient, so they gave her subcutaneous fluids and antibiotics. That vet became our normal vet from that day forward because they took such great care of Nala. She made a great recovery but her paw was severely swollen for a while. After the swelling subsided, she was fully recovered and was on the road to living a happy, healthy life. She got sick a few times after this altercation, but since she almost died, I always pay special attention to her and ensure she gets treatment immediately. We never know when she might get that ill again, and to this day, we still do not know what she was sick with. Nala was the beginning of something much bigger. She was the inspiration for me starting my animal rescue. Nala was a rescue, and I noticed a lot of other cats needed help, too.

CHAPTER FOURTEEN

A Turning Point

July 2022

My rescue stemmed from the start of an *Instagram* post and grew from there. It was originally called The Devoted Petz, but I recently rebranded to something more personal and a better representation of myself. While Jake and I were on our honeymoon (finally!) in Montana, I rebranded and changed the name to Ever Greene Rescue and Rehabilitation. My *Instagram*'s goal was for our personal animals to be a voice for others in need. Our mission was to help all animals in need whether big or small, and I threw myself into it quickly. After gaining some followers on *Instagram* and doing a lot of research, I received my first big fundraiser partner. I partnered with Pals Socks and sold purposefully mismatched socks right before Christmas, and they were a hit. I was able to sell 109 pairs of socks, 9 gift sets, and $263 was donated separately. This all added up to $898 for my first fundraiser. That was a big accomplishment for one person. I raised all of that money on my own through direct marketing. The money did not last very long, regrettably.

I used it for medical expenses on the multiple cats I rescued. I had to get vaccines, spay/neuter, buy supplies, heal some from sickness, and put one down. Part of my rescue journey included putting down a five-week-old kitten who was septic and fighting for her life. I had to make the decision to put her out of her misery and let her drift off into peace. This was the right decision, but it was not a cheap one. My funds were drained quickly, but I made it work through other small fundraisers and some of my personal money.

Jake and I loved Nala so much, we decided to look into getting more animals. We both grew up with dachshunds and decided two small dogs would be perfect in our first home together. We decided to wait on a big dog until we got a yard, whenever that would be. After we decided, I started my difficult search. Purebred dachshunds were hard to find at affordable prices because most are American Kennel Club (AKC) bred and can cost upwards of 1,500 dollars or more. I searched for a while, and ran into a lot of problems. I could not find one that stuck out to me. They were too expensive, too far, or they were a scam. I faced a lot of potential scams but I knew what to look out for and always caught on before sending any money and letting them win. I mainly searched websites and *Craigslist,* but was not successful.

A few weeks in, I switched to *Facebook* and joined a few dachshund groups. After a few days in the group, I found a breeder with a litter that caught my eye. He had a litter with a couple dapples, and one blue and cream dapple stood out to Jake and me. There was one issue, this breeder was located in Washington and we lived in California. Jake and I did the math and even with a round trip ticket to Washington and the fee for the puppy, it would still be less than any other one closer we had found. We told the breeder we were all in and started paying for the puppy, put a deposit down, and I started planning my flights. Bo's gotcha day was set for September 26th, 2020, and I was ready for another adventure. It was a long day of traveling but I got a lot of work done and did not have to spend any extra money for lodging since we were leaving the same day.

When I arrived at the airport, I headed outside to the pickup area where I met Bo's breeder. We talked for a little bit and then I took him inside in his carrier. I completed some work on my computer, played with Bo, and then we boarded our flight. Bo behaved very good on the flight and when we got home, Jake picked us up.

We had a great few first weeks with Bo, but his breeder had another litter born shortly after and we decided on getting our second dachshund, Nemo, from that litter. Bo and Nemo are in fact related - we believe Bo is Nemo's uncle. I picked Nemo up about a month later, and the day was very similar to when I got Bo. When we got home, Bo was ecstatic to be a big brother. Nala has always had motherly tendencies and she would constantly groom, hug, and mother the boys when they were babies. With one cat and two dogs, our house was in harmony. We did not get anymore animals for a while that were technically ours, but we had house guests while I was doing my rescue work.

Everything in my life seemed great for a bit, but then things drastically changed and I had to make another hard decision.

For the few weeks leading up to when I left to get Bo, I was messaging my mom and telling her my plans and how excited I was. Every time we would chat, she would ask me if I was sure it was not a scam and that she was worried. I would reassure her each time I knew it was not because I know the signs to look out for. We had been potentially scammed many times prior. I knew my mom meant well but having to answer the same question five times in a row was very exasperating and I became irritated. Things were better for a while, but I confided in Jake multiple times about how I was upset. My mom did not trust I knew what I was doing, and it did not sit right with me. He suggested I talk to them about my concerns because it might help, but it made things worse.

CHAPTER FIFTEEN

A Talk of Change

August 2020 to April 2021

At first, I was not going to say anything about my frustrations, but my family and I had not been getting along for a while. One day, I randomly decided it was time to voice my concerns and I sent them a group text. This sadly backfired. I sent a decently long text, voicing my frustrations and how I thought I deserved an apology. My parents' reaction was not positive. They came back bombarding me with accusations. They said I should stop complaining and they were going to tell my family how ungrateful I was, along with many other unnecessary, hateful things. All I wanted was an apology, which I never demanded. Instead, I got to have a meltdown in my car for an hour because something I said was so skewed with their response, I just lost it, and that was the last straw. I told them about my meltdown, and my messages were ignored. I decided enough was enough and I called Jake to ask if I could switch to T-Mobile and join his plan. After work, Jake met me at T-Mobile and I switched over. When we got home, I transferred all of my data from my old phone to my new one. After I was done, I did something I never wanted to do and blocked my parents on my new phone.

Blocking my parents was one of the most difficult things I had to do but it was the right thing for my mental health. I could not handle the emotional turmoil I had been experiencing anymore and I had to cut ties at that point. Not talking to my parents for a few months was hard, but I felt at peace for a while. I took some time to myself, but started reaching out to my parents slowly on *Facebook* messenger. Reaching out was hard; our relationship was broken in my mind and I did not know where to begin in order to fix it.

I do not recall all our conversations on *Facebook* but I do know we talked about going to family therapy. Family therapy was a great idea, but it did not go well. A few weeks later, Jake and I headed over to my parents' house in the morning for therapy and I was a ball of nerves. Our session was not a positive experience, because whenever I would talk, I would be interrupted so I decided to interrupt my mom while she was talking. That was not a great decision on either of our parts. While I was interrupting, my dad lost it and screamed in my face to shut up. I ran out of the room, crying, and jumped into our car.

Jake stayed a few minutes after me and caught the closing thoughts of the therapist. She suggested to my parents that my mental disorder caused me to skew information and make up scenarios that were not true. Which led my parents to believe the issues I was having were not true and I had made them up. When Jake came to the car and told me that, I was very disturbed. Now I had to deal with the potential of being blamed for every issue we had in our relationship again even though I was not the sole problem.

My dad apologized later on, and things seemed better. My parents told me they planned to continue to see that therapist and I would go to mine. We would work on our issues separately and then come together for family therapy. My parents never went to therapy. They said they would, but decided not to since the therapist said I made all of the scenarios up in my head.

I continued my therapy sessions, and my psychiatrist told me what that therapist said to them was untrue. She told me I may have made things up in my head at the beginning of my recovery, but not at that point because I had made such good progress. I still yearned to make things better.

My parents invited us to family Thanksgiving because they thought we were all ready to come back together as a family. I did not think we were ready, but Jake convinced me to go. I hoped for the best but still expected the worst. The night did not go well. I wanted to hang out with Jake most of the night because I was not fully comfortable around my family yet. But my sister and mom told me to leave Jake alone and let him hang out with my dad, which I did not like. Their dog ended up attacking/biting one of my puppies as well which severely upset me and everyone else played down my concerns. That night did not end well in my opinion, but I feel like things could have been handled differently on everyone's end. My reactions could have been different and their comments and concerns could have been more understanding as well. I do not know how my family's night ended, but mine ended in tears and a mental breakdown.

At that point in my life, I was trying to figure out who I was as a person. I did not want to be disrespected, and I believe respect was earned not given. I understand my parents are my parents, they always will be, but that did not give them the right to blatantly be disrespectful to me.

The first few times we went over to their house after we had started talking again were very hard. Each time would end with me in tears, and breakdowns when Jake and I got home. Jake told me I had a choice each time to either kick them out of my life for good or learn to live with it. I never wanted to cut ties with my family completely, having a relationship at that time was extremely hard on my mental health, but I still wanted to attempt it. I decided to try and find ways to cope when we would talk or hang out, and then things started to get better. We would not fight as much and my parents would not say damaging things as often but those instances were still there. I had to learn how to cope with things on my own and decompartmentalize in order to have the relationship I wanted, even though it did seem very broken at times. Sometimes it seemed my parents did not put in the same effort to fix our relationship while I still made the necessary steps to try and keep my peace and be a part of my family.

Our relationships started getting better, but I realized my relationship with Jake had been slipping. Although I loved my family, we did not have the same relationship Jake had with his family. I grew up my whole life barely seeing my dad because he was deployed all the time or on workups. Whereas Jake grew up seeing everyone every day, including his mom and all his cousins, grandparents, and extended family. Our upbringing was very different in that way. I do not regret the way I was raised, I enjoyed my childhood, but this made me blind to how negatively not seeing his family was affecting Jake.

CHAPTER SIXTEEN

A New Adventure

April 2021

One night, we got into an argument and I had an epiphany. He was miserable because of how terribly he missed his family. Up until that point, we were planning on staying in San Diego and trying to move somewhere else and sell our condominium. But our plans changed that night and we decided to start preparing to move to the east coast when he left the service a few months later. I realized with my upbringing I would be okay without seeing my family all the time. I am sad sometimes and I do miss them terribly, but I am not miserable and, strangely enough, I presume it has helped our relationship. Living on the east coast again has also substantially improved my mental health. Even though I do not have many friends yet, I have noticed how my surroundings have positively affected my overall outlook on life. And I am building more of a community here every day.

Moving across the country was not easy. There were a ton of questions to answer and a lot of preparation to do. We wondered where we would live, how we would get there, if we could take all of our animals, and a bunch of other questions. We discussed for a bit and decided to move to East Tennessee. The exact location was still undetermined, but the general vicinity was going to be around Knoxville Tennessee. Next, we had to decide how we would get there, and plan where we would live. For a while, we thought about buying a house, buying land, and building a house, or buying an RV to live in for a while. Our biggest issue was trying to figure all of this out while we lived across the country.

We decided our best course of action was for me to leave before him and try to get everything set up and then to fly back and drive out together. We settled on this decision and I started making preparations. My first focus was getting a job lined up, which I did in a few days. My mom had mentioned *Amazon* warehouse jobs and how easy they were to get into, and

I decided to try it out. I went on the website and applied, I took a short assessment, passed, and then received a job offer.

Everything had been working out. I even found an apartment to sublet for the few months I was going to be there alone. All I had left to do was choose a date to leave. My sister was getting married on April 11th and I was excited to be there for that. I decided to leave on April 14th, which gave me time to focus on my sister's wedding, pack up my things, and have time to relax before my big move. I was starting work at *Amazon* on the 28th, and had a social media manager position lined up. Life was great and everything was working out. On April 14th I woke up, got ready, and said my heartfelt goodbyes to Jake because I had no idea when I would see him again, and I officially left California on another one of my life adventures.

I had come up with a plan to finish my cross-country trek in six days. I left on the fourteenth and planned to arrive on the twentieth. I had to let my apartment complex know my estimated arrival date to get my keys, unpack, and settle in before starting my full-time job at *Amazon*. Even though Austin Texas was a bit out of my way, I planned to stop in Texas to visit my family for a few days in the middle of my trip. My first stop was planned for Las Cruces, New Mexico, which was only about ten hours from San Diego. The first part of my trip was very easy, and I made it to Las Cruces around six in the evening on my first day. I checked into my hotel, unpacked, showered, ate dinner, and performed some work for my social media position, and then headed to sleep to prepare for the next day.

I arrived at Gram's house around eight at night the next day, and she had ordered dinner for us to go pick up. When we lived in San Diego, there was a lot of food and restaurants that were always a treat for us to go to because they were not located in San Diego. One of these treats included Mr. Gatti's Pizza, which my whole family loved, so we decided on pizza that night.

I spent most of my few days there just relaxing, but I was able to see my mom's extended family and some more of my dad's. After a few days, I left well rested and ready to continue my adventure.

Once I got close to Arkansas, I realized something. I had a gaming friend I met online who lived in Arkansas. I decided to message her and see if we could have gotten together. As luck would have it, I was staying in Little Rock Arkansas and I was close enough to be able to see her, her husband, their baby, and her other friend. I arrived at my hotel, checked in, relaxed a little bit, and got ready to leave. I ran a quick errand and then went to meet them about halfway at a Texas Roadhouse. It was a wonderful night, and I was excited to meet them.

After dinner, I went back to the hotel, went to sleep, and prepared for my last day of traveling. I was on the road for less than an hour when something frightful happened. I was driving decently fast down the highway and I hit a pothole, instantly popping my tire. My tread was completely torn off and I had no idea of what to do. I got to the nearest exit and parked at a gas station and called for a tow truck. I was not very excited about it, but another adventure was set to begin.

I waited at the gas station for a few hours before my tow truck arrived. The gentleman who picked me up was very sweet. I forgot his real name, but his nickname was Lunchbox. He gave me the nickname Red. We drove around for a bit, trying to find tires that were my size. Eventually, we found a shop that had mine in stock. It only took about twenty to thirty minutes for them to put my tires on and then I was back on the road. This put a dent in my plans, but I was still arriving in Knoxville at a decent time.

The rest of my trip went very smoothly, and I was ecstatic to move into my new, short-term home. My room was a bit dingy; the apartment complex did a very good job of staging rooms to look clean on the website. My room had mold, the bathroom had black mold, and the walls had holes. Either way, it was okay because my room was only temporary. I left to get some supplies for my room at *Walmart* one day to make it look nicer, and then I went home to decorate. I got some pillows, a memory foam pad for my bed, some candles, and a few decorative things to put around the room. Once that was done and it was a bit better, I took a few days to relax before my first day of work.

Working at *Amazon* was fun for a bit, but it was hard. I was not getting a lot of sleep because the people above me would make noise throughout the night and it was hard for me to relax and fall asleep. I made it work and stayed at *Amazon* for a while.

Between working at Amazon and my social media manager position, I started planning on where we should live and what type of home we would get. After a bit, we settled on buying a home that was already built and had a decent amount of land.

I found a realtor fairly quick. Crazily enough, she moved to the Knoxville area a while back from a city close to where we lived in San Diego. We applied for a loan with a lender she knew. It took a bit to get approved but only because we had to wait on a letter of employment for Jake. Once we got the letter from *Amazon*, where Jake was going to work as well, we were approved for a loan within a couple days, and were finally able to start shopping.

I found a couple I was interested in, but they did not work out. One specific house stood out to me, just like our first house. I reached out to my realtor about the house, and she said it would possibly be difficult to get, because the house was being sold independently and it had been on the market for a while. I pushed her a bit and we decided to look at the house as soon as possible.

My drive out there was beautiful, and as soon as we stepped in, I had the same feeling about this house as our first. This house was meant to be our second home, and I was determined to make it happen. The house was far from perfect, but the land was worth it and we had all the space we wanted. Now that I knew the house I wanted Jake and me to move into, it was time to try and convince Jake to let me buy a house without him. It took a bit of time, but I ultimately convinced him to let me pursue the house, and my realtor and I put in an offer. All we had left to do was wait and see if our offer was accepted.

We were able to get early occupancy and move in as soon as Jake and I arrived. Things seemed to be going well. But that was not the case. We were having issues from the start. Our power was not on the first night, so we had to rough it. We had no water the first week or so, which made living a bit hard. Eventually, we got it figured out but not without more issues. We had water, but our water heater was not working and we had a pipe burst. Luckily, we did not own the house yet and the seller was able to fix everything. But it was still a pain to deal with. Eventually, everything was fixed, and we believed as if it was smooth sailing from there. We were wrong. We had a buyer lined up for our house in San Diego for a while, but they were having issues getting approved for a loan to finish the purchase.

Jake and I did not understand why for a while but we got a hard awakening one day while I was at work. My realtor messaged me with some bad news; our buyers had backed out and were no longer purchasing the house. It was difficult for them to be approved for the loan because our HOA for the condominium had depleted their reserves from around 1 million to 15,000. Because of this, lenders would only accept loans who had 20% down or more to help protect themselves. Finding individuals with loans in that manner was difficult in a military town. VA loans were very common in military towns, and they required 0% down. This put a damper in our plans of selling our house and put us into panic mode.

CHAPTER SEVENTEEN

A New Challenge

Our life for the next few months was complete hell, and it has not let up much since. We were in a constant fear of being homeless and not knowing what would happen if our house was unable to sell. We had to continue to pay our mortgage in San Diego as well as our early occupancy rent in Madisonville. I had to pay a few extra months for the apartment room I rented as well. This caused us to get into a huge amount of debt in order to stay afloat.

There was one thing keeping us sane, which was our big wedding celebration coming up in October of 2021 which we worked hard to still make happen, with help from our family as well.

Jake and I had a small wedding and were married rather quickly before he left on a seven-month deployment. We had a ceremony and a dinner at our small wedding but not any of the extra celebrations that occur at a wedding. We were set to have our big wedding celebration with my amazing expensive dress, a nice dinner, father-daughter dance, mother-son dance, speeches, the whole shebang. This wedding was the only thing keeping us sane during our life troubles, and we were determined to make it happen.

Our dreadful life began to adversely affect my health and my ability to work. For a very long time, I had been taking a medicine called lithium but it had reverse effects on me for a while, which I did not start to notice until our life took a drastic turn. Lithium caused me to not have bladder control, and I lost over half of my head of hair, but I started to notice additional side effects. One morning, I was driving to *Amazon* and started to have a panic attack; one of many. I was driving and my head started to become cloudy. I was going in and out of consciousness and could not function properly. I feel I was experiencing derealization again. Somehow, by the grace of God, I was able to text Jake and let him know. I was able to pull off the highway and park at a gas station to try and calm myself down. It helped some, and I got back on the road so I was not late for work. By the time I arrived at work, I was still not feeling well. I went inside and told our nurse on campus to call an ambulance for me. By the time the ambulance arrived, I had calmed down a bit, but I still wanted to go to the hospital. By the time I arrived, I was still pretty calm. The hospital staff performed an exam on me and said everything was fine. I knew I was still slipping in and out of consciousness, but never actually passed out. It is hard to explain, but my vision basically went cloudy and it felt like tunnel vision.

While I was lying in the hospital bed, I slipped out of consciousness, and I called for help. By the time they got to me, though, I was fine.

This is one of the reasons why it is hard to understand mental health. Many individuals do not understand the complexity of a mental disorder. Unfortunately, not all hospitals understand mental disorders fully either, unless they specialize in them.

A few hours later, I was discharged and still not feeling 100%. I called my mom to talk to her about what happened while I was waiting for Jake to come get me. My head hurt, I was not feeling well in general, the world seemed very dark and dreary, and I still had my weird cloudy tunnel vision.

After Jake picked me up, things slowly got better, and I was fully recovered later on that day. Things were okay for a while, but I would have more panic attacks at home that were similar. I would be sitting down somewhere or lying in bed and my body would tense up and basically start seizing. I never had actual seizures but it would be hard to move, breathe, speak, or think. During these times, I spoke as if I was a toddler at some points.

Although this does sound bad, I was not close to being in psychosis. I never had a huge fear of that. My anxiety was through the roof and caused my body to go into panic mode. There were a few instances where an incident similar to the one when I was driving to *Amazon* occurred again. One night, Jake and I went to a rodeo to try and forget for a night how terrible our life was at the time. But we ended up in a hospital again at the end of the night. Eventually, the panic attacks stopped. I learned to relax and just let life take its course. I learned how to do something that has been hard for me my entire life, to live and let go. I could not control the situation, but it was severely affecting me negatively. I had to learn to cope, stay strong, and keep my sanity. I made a decision to live life for the day instead of trying to control every detail, because I saw how negatively being a control freak was affecting me.

All the chaos in my life caused me to miss my family in San Diego. I was grateful for their help and wanted to do something nice in return, so I concocted a plan. *Amazon* was giving out bonuses to their employees who worked there throughout the pandemic, and I was going to use my bonus to buy a ticket to San Diego at the end of August for my mom's birthday. I texted them and cunningly found out all their plans in order to surprise them successfully. They were going to a winery I had been to before on the night I was flying in, which made surprising everyone easy.

I flew into Los Angeles because it was cheaper and rented a car then drove to my best friend's house to get dressed up for dinner.

When I arrived at the winery, my sister's husband spotted me first, but he did not say anything. I had a video recording and I snuck up behind my mom and surprised her. She was so happy. I stopped the recording before my dad saw me, but he started crying. He can be a big softy at times. All in all, the surprise went great and I was happy to spend a few days in San Diego with them.

After I got home from my trip, things started falling into place slowly. There were ups and downs. We would get good news and have hope, only to find out two or three days later things were messed up again. We would pay one bill and be great, then the next day something else would come up or an emergency would happen where we would be back at square one.

Jake and I had a lot of different jobs. I worked at an airport, and did contract work for *Hertz*, but I did not stay for long periods of time. One day when I was driving from my *Hertz* job to *Coca Cola* for an interview, I hit a pothole. I popped a tire yet again and had to pay over five hundred dollars for a new pair. This occurrence set Jake and I back again, but we continued to carry on.

We were able to officially purchase our home on July 13th 2021. There was a lot of back and forth, but our realtors went above and beyond for us. One crucial thing to buying our house here was selling our house in California, but that was becoming difficult. Our realtor pulled out all his big guns and had a buyer lined up for us. In July of 2021, before what I like to call "judgement day," Jake and I left our house to go stay in a nearby hotel in Sweetwater, Tennessee. Staying in our house that night would have just been too hard and extremely depressing for us. We could have been homeless the next day with no other options in sight at the time. The next day, we went to a jeweler to sell one of my rings because we thought we would need the money. Within five minutes of sitting down, I got a text that our house had officially sold! We were ecstatic, but we still sold my ring and spent some of the money to celebrate. God really is gracious. He provided everything we needed in the nick of time.

It took Jake and me a while to get out of deep waters but at least we have a roof over our heads and food on our table, and we are on our way to recovering.

There were a few things I did that helped keep us afloat for a while. I found a Facebook advertisement for a job as a production assistant with the rate of $200 a day. I did not expect the posting to be real, but thought it wouldn't hurt to apply. I received a call from the coordinator about ten minutes later and was offered the position. I enjoyed the job and was happy to be a part of the team; I started to look for another production gig to line up for when that job ended. I found another one, but it was in Atlanta and would wrap a few days before mine and Jake's big wedding celebration. I was offered the job, and the coordinator and I decided we would figure out all of the details later. I was ecstatic and posted my good news on Facebook, informing all my family and friends.

My mom commented on my status, asking if I would be home in time for the wedding, and I assured her that I would. She then proceeded to text me and ask again to make sure I would be there before the wedding. I think my comment saying I would be there before everyone got there was not a definitive enough answer, so she felt as if she needed to text me while I was working for more confirmation. I repeated what I had said yet again, but it was not enough. She then proceeded to call me manipulative and ungrateful because I was not able to give a straight answer.

I said I would be home before everyone got there, and it should have been left at that. I am an adult. I can be trusted to be where I need to be, when I need to be there, and am not required to give exact answers to anyone.

I asked for an explanation as to why my answer was not good enough. My mother responded in a childish and harmful manner with the statement, "If you can't figure that out, your brain and the way you think needs help." This was very hurtful to me, and I instantly burst into tears on set. I was alone and had a few minutes to pull myself together before anyone saw me. A statement such as that one was very damaging to someone who had come so far in recovery. She then proceeded to threaten to not come to our wedding, and I was done at that point, so I said, "okay," hoping to move on and focus on my work. I did not want to fight any more; it was not worth it. Jake stepped in shortly after and then things were resolved. I can see her side, as to why I should have been able to give a straight-forward answer, but the nasty comment about my brain and the way I think needing help was extremely uncalled for in my opinion. My mom and I had more similar fights like those, but we both moved forward and apologized rather quickly. Our relationship has substantially improved in the last year, and I am grateful for that. After the wedding, our relationship started getting much better. My family is one of the most important things to me, and I do not want to experience another falling out.

I had a great time on my next job. I was in Atlanta for four days. The production was set for Monday through Friday, but we worked things out and I was able to help out until Thursday instead. Each day was packed full of fun. Our first day on set, one of the venues we were planning to film at backed out and we were all frantically searching for a new one. I was a part of this search crew and I happened to find a nice place, but it was a bit outside of the city, so I chose not to pursue it at the time.

A few hours went by and no one had found a suitable venue yet. I decided to take a chance. I pulled up the venue I found on my laptop and went over to show the director, and he was surprisingly interested. Despite the fact it was kind of far outside of the city, he said it might have been nice to get away for the day. Now that the interest was there, we had to call and check for availability, and we were lucky enough that it was available the whole day we needed the site. There was a choice between the venue I found and another, and two people left shortly after to go scout the venues.

When they returned, one guy hopped out of the car and said, "Whoever found this place saved our asses." I just happened to be outside at the right time and was able to raise my hand and politely say, "That was me. I found it!." I drove home Thursday afternoon after we wrapped to greet Jake and his parents so our wedding weekend could finally begin. Shortly before our wedding, I decided to try something new to help repair my relationship with my mother. My mom and I had a tendency to assume a text message or statement was meant to be rude when in reality it was not. I decided the resolution started with me, and I needed to take the necessary steps to protect my peace. I began to take potentially rude messages from my family with a grain of salt. Instead of assuming the text was rude and getting angry, I would let it slide and just say okay and/or change the subject. This one small change on my end has substantially improved the relationship I have with my mother, and I am grateful for that. I hope my change will eventually rub off and our relationship will continue to improve.

The wedding-packed weekend was perfect. I enjoyed seeing my mom and we had no quarrels all weekend. It was very enjoyable. A lot of things did go wrong, but the experience was unforgettably amazing.

CHAPTER EIGHTEEN

A Positive Switch

October 2021

Our wedding was the only thing keeping Jake and I sane throughout our whole house debacle, and it was finally happening. Jake and I had gotten married rather quickly about two years prior, but we were finally having our large celebration with a big cake, first dances, saying our own vows, and a big dinner with an after party. Except, while the party was big, our audience was still small. No more than thirty people attended, and more than half were a part of our wedding party. It was very big and special in our hearts. All of Jake's brothers but one were in the wedding. Jake's dad and PawPaw performed our ceremony since we were already married, and all the grandmothers were flower girls. My uncle stepped in as my ring bearer since the original was unable to make it. Jake decided to play guitar and sing a song as I walked down the aisle as well, which was the best part.

Our wedding was perfect, and the next day, we flew off to Montana for a week to celebrate our honeymoon. I had posted on *Facebook* about where we were staying a few weeks prior to us leaving. One of my childhood friends messaged me because she knew it was their hometown from the look of the sky and we were able to save some money by borrowing their car and visiting with them a few nights. We went fly fishing, visited a museum, relaxed a lot, ate really good food, and visited Yellowstone. Our honeymoon was perfect.

A few weeks after being back in Tennessee, I received notice of an interview for a project team position with *Walmart*. My interview went well. While waiting on news for *Walmart,* I did some other small production gigs and brought some more money in. I looked into working close to home for a bit, but nothing ever worked out.

I figured out how to use a lot of different cash advance apps that help you manage money and keep yourself on track. Those apps helped Jake and I significantly to ensure our family was taken care of.

Eventually, I received a random email and text message from *Walmart* stating I had received the project position. Honestly, I had forgotten I even applied and interviewed. I was very excited, and started looking more into the job, telling everyone how excited I was and stopped looking for other jobs. Little did I know I would not hear from any live person from *Walmart* until a few days before my orientation. This month or so of uncertainty caused me to have a lot of anxiety. I started developing more health problems. I was constantly cold, no matter what I did, and would experience aches and pains. I would have random numbness in my extremities, I was exhausted out of the blue, head fog, headaches, and sometimes would experience sleep paralysis. I felt terrible every day and had no idea why. Then I looked at the constant in my life and realized my medicine was the culprit and making me literally ill.

When I realized what my medicine was doing to my body, I decided I had enough and was going to quit Lithium. I chose to slowly taper off and try alternative methods. I chose to try to regulate my bipolar on my own and with CBD, but I had to fully get off Lithium in order to do that. If CBD and Lithium are mixed it can cause Lithium toxicity, which I did not want to risk since it was already affecting me so negatively. I told my psychiatrist at our next appointment about my plan, and she agreed tapering off Lithium was the right choice.

We started the process, and it took about three months but I finally stopped Lithium. I feel much healthier, no brain fog, I can think clearly, and I can finally experience and regulate my emotions again. Although I originally wanted to try to use CBD to regulate my bipolar, my psychiatrist and I decided I was going to regulate it with as needed medicine. She prescribed me Seroquel to help with sleep as needed and then hydroxyzine to regulate my anxiety.

Now that I am able to make out my emotions again, I can easily tell when I am on edge and need a bit of help. When these feelings come, I take my hydroxyzine and am calmed down within half an hour. I have found ways to regulate my mood naturally as well. I can tell when I need to breathe a bit deeper or go outside and get some fresh air. Having the ability to identify and deal with my emotions again has given me the privilege to regulate them on my own.

Jake and I accrued some more debt while I was waiting to hear from *Walmart*. I was fortunate enough to receive one more production gig in North Carolina while on standby. These production gigs are nice and extra money is always great, but they do take a while to get the money to you sometimes. After I started working at *Walmart*, I realized something. All the extra ways I was finding money just stopped and it became harder to find those opportunities. I was always told, and I also believe, God will provide somehow. I determined my means of getting extra income ceased because God knew I would be starting at *Walmart* soon and would not need the extra cash. The extra cash would have been nice, but he was right. I do not even have the time to work the extra jobs. Working at *Walmart* is great. I really enjoy my team and the job is fun. I was hired at the tail end of a project and was not able to see the process from start to finish, but the new *Walmarts* look fantastic.

Jake had a lot of different job options as well. He picked a company in North Carolina that other members of his family worked at to apply to. Jake applied for the position and received an interview. A week or so later, he went off to North Carolina for a drug test. On his way back, his check engine light came on and he gave me a call to let me know. I was at work at the time, but I left early to go and help him. I was ten minutes away from where he was waiting and a pothole came out of nowhere and I popped a tire, yet again. There we were in the middle of nowhere with no idea of what to do. We had just paid all our other bills and were completely dried up from our expenses. Luckily, my parents were able to help us out and we spent a couple hours going to get my tire changed, putting oil in Jake's car, and then finally heading home after yet another unexpected expense that derailed our plans. Although this would have been a great job opportunity and he could have seen his family a lot more, Jake ultimately decided to not take the position. He chose to stay at home with me because I had just started tapering off my Lithium and it was important for me to not be alone.

We decided not too long before that that it was time for us to start going to church. We had gone a couple times, and I thought about asking the pastor if he knew of any potential jobs. He had a job for Jake lined up the very next day.

Jake really enjoyed his new job, but luck ran out and he was let go due to missing too many days. Jake's PawPaw who officiated the wedding had passed away and he had to miss a decent amount of work to attend his funeral. His job gave him a specific day to return and he could not make it back in time. When Jake returned from the funeral he was met with a termination notice.

When Jake's grandfather was in the hospital, I remember his family chatting about what he was experiencing.

The doctors had given him Ativan, and he had been aggressive, as well as believing he was going to be in a commercial. I could not help but notice the similarities between what his grandfather was going through and my own experience with psychosis. I mentioned to them that maybe they should request a psych eval for his grandfather because it might help. My suggestion was not taken well and I ended up leaving the group chat shortly after. I understand why they were upset; it was not the right place or time for me to try and diagnose his grandfather, even though I was just trying to give support in my own way.

I called my mother afterward and let her know. She agreed I should not have made the comment, but was proud of me for recognizing the similarities.

I learned something new that day. Apparently, ICU psychosis, also known as delirium, is a common occurrence in patients who are near death. Now I am worried whenever I may die, that I will go into psychosis again. It is a good thing I inform all of my doctors about my psychotic break.

Since Tennessee is a right-to-work state, we are able to quit for any reason and can be fired for any reason. Jake was upset when he was fired but I assured him it would be okay as long as he got a job soon. We were finally in a good spot financially, and I owe that all to God because I do believe our life started turning around when we started going to church again.

It was not long after Jake was fired, that I had to quit at *Walmart*. I enjoyed working at *Walmart* but working nights was very hard on my body and mind. I had to quit because I was injured while stocking in dairy and sent home. Corporate *Walmart* has their attendance system set up in a way that even though I was sent home, unless my Leave of Absence (LOA) was approved, I would get a negative point. Unfortunately, my LOA was not approved and before I was fired, I decided to quit because it would look better on me in the end. It did not take long for me to start another job, so Jake and I are still doing well.

We may not go to church every single day, but I do hope we continue to go as much as we can because of all the blessings we have received. Jake and I were very lucky because we qualified for Covid assistance on our mortgage. Since our Covid assistance began, we have been able to save money and are finally getting back on our feet. Right before I left *Walmart*, we were blessed with some great news. Jake is going to be receiving his disability check from the Marine Corps and it is enough to cover our mortgage and a few other bills. We are taking proper precautions every day to continue to build a better future for ourselves.

CHAPTER NINETEEN

The Facts

As a young girl, I never knew exactly what was wrong with me. I was very hyper and sometimes had an issue focusing. A physician told my parents I had ADHD, although there was a strong possibility it was not true. When I was a young girl, I was part of a statistic, the statistic of young girls who are misdiagnosed ADHD when, in reality, they are bipolar.

In the early twentieth century, physicians would not diagnose children with bipolar disorder. Back in 1975, when Elizabeth Weller was practicing as a resident, there was no belief bipolar disorder existed in children. Weller is a professor of psychiatry and pediatrics as well as the vice chair of psychiatry at the University of Pennsylvania School of Medicine. She stated that doctors believed in that time period that "normal childhood behavior was sort of hypomanic". One hundred or so years later and there is still resistance to diagnosing bipolar disorder in children. How bipolar presents itself in children is different from adults. Children will become more irritable and will have a decreased need for sleep. Individual children with bipolar will usually be able to function effectively on barely any sleep. Weller says, "getting the diagnosis correct… leads to the correct treatment pathway".[1]

It is important for the general public to have a better understanding of mental health. Many people believe those who commit suicide had a choice but that is usually not the case. Our brains naturally will not let us end our lives; our fight or flight would naturally kick in to save ourselves. Those who commit suicide often have a chemical imbalance in their brain which allows them to successfully end their lives. Mental health activist Kevin Hines is taking action to help prevent suicides. Hines is one of very few to have survived a jump off the famous

---

[1] Rosack, J., (2002, July 5). *Bipolar Disorder Often Misdiagnosed In Children, Expert Says*. Psychiatric News. Retrieved April 13, 2022, from https://psychnews.psychiatryonline.org/doi/full/10.1176/pn.37.13.0026

Golden Gate Bridge in San Francisco. Hines suffered from many mental issues including psychosis, depression, paranoia, and hallucinations. Hines stated a voice in his head compelled him to jump and die. When the voice said, "Jump now," he leaped over the railing and began the 75 mile per hour free fall. Hines instantly regretted his decision and fought to save his life. His fall crushed three of his spinal vertebrae and broke his ankle. Hines cried out to God, saying he made a mistake and did not want to die. Until the Coast Guard was able to come rescue him, a sea lion kept Hines above the surface of the water so he was able to breathe. Seven months after his jump, Hines began to tell his story. His first talk was to middle schoolers.

A few weeks after his talk, he received letters from the children saying his talk had made a difference in their lives. He decided to tell his story, "anyway, anywhere [he] can"[2] in order

---

[2] Article by: Diane Herbst. (2021, May 20). *Kevin Hines jumped off the Golden Gate Bridge, and survived.* Psycom.net - Mental Health Treatment Resource Since 1996. Retrieved April 15, 2022, from

to help those who struggle and empower them to seek help. Mental health activist Kevin Hines urges anyone who sees someone suffering to reach out. We'll never know when our actions might save a life. Mental health is still widely understudied and misunderstood.

Jake and I go on road trips often, and he always puts on serial killer podcasts, which we listen to closely. There have been multiple times I noticed similarities in their diagnosis to my own. The stories we heard about these serial killers mentioned schizophrenia, psychosis, and mood disorders. Their disorders were often developed from trauma filled childhoods. Since mental health is widely understudied, our society is potentially failing these individuals before they are even given a proper chance for a quality life. Those of sound mind usually would not commit a crime, murder, or end their lives. If our society spent more time focusing on the reform of mental health, there may be less suicides, less murder, and less crime.

---

https://www.psycom.net/kevin-hines-survived-golden-gate-bridge-suicide/

There are societal beliefs surrounding those who commit crimes, do drugs, or even commit suicide to be a menace. Although this may be true, it is not always the case. We should not be quick to judge the person we see talking to themselves on the street corner. What if that person is fighting a battle inside their minds they are unable to escape? We should not judge the person we see holding a gun to their head and crying. What if their brain gave up and cannot hold on anymore? We need to do better. We need to learn how to recognize when someone needs help and offer our support instead of judgement.

There is a typical judgement surrounding mental health. Many people believe mental health is a weakness, and means those who suffer are lesser than and cannot do the same things others can, which is damaging to those fighting in the battle against their own minds. The stigma around mental health being a weakness can often make the disorder worse and recovery more difficult. This stigma around mental health makes it tough for men who suffer from mental illness to seek help as well. Men are taught from a young age to not cry, showing emotions is weak, and to just be a man, which can be dangerous. This stigma can cause men to not seek help and bottle up their feelings, which may be lethal in the end.[3] Humanity should not be quick to judge those with a mental illness. We are not lesser than. Our brains are just wired different.

Young children, adolescents, and adults alike are susceptible to misdiagnosis, which is cause for concern.

Even though a misdiagnosis can be detrimental, it is not always the case. My misdiagnosis was not deadly. It was beneficial in a way. However, I was left to live with the repercussions of a traumatic brain experience (TBE) after my psychotic break. Some of the effects of my TBE include memory loss. My memory is very strange and selective. I can recall almost every negative memory I have, but do not have a huge recollection of good memories. I cannot remember most of my adolescent life either. I remember very specific things,

---

[3] Article by: Diane Herbst. (2021, May 20). *Kevin Hines jumped off the Golden Gate Bridge, and survived.* Psycom.net - Mental Health Treatment Resource Since 1996. Retrieved April 15, 2022, from https://www.psycom.net/kevin-hines-survived-golden-gate-bridge-suicide/

such as something my husband said a week ago because he argued with me about it that day and I had to prove him wrong. My TBE severely increased the intensity of my sensory overload (SO). I have always had issues with certain sounds and too much of them, but it seems my SO is a lot worse since recovering. Before my psychotic break, I never had headaches. I do not get headaches all the time currently, but I get them more frequently than before the break. Any loud sound these days can trigger a headache, it seems, but they do not occur every time, thankfully.

I noticed I am much more sensitive to light as well. When I worked nights and drove more frequently at night rather than the day, I caught myself often wincing while I drove and even holding my breath from the discomfort. I do not know why I had that reaction. It may be because my brain is more sensitive now or a side effect from when I thought I was going into the light before I went into psychosis. Either way, I am taking necessary steps to make driving at night more enjoyable, and went to the eye doctor and received a new prescription and glasses, thanks to my Gram.

I have never been close to another psychotic break and for that, I am grateful. I live every day of my life trying to improve who I am as an individual and putting my mental health first. I only have one life to live, and this is my second chance to live it right.

CHAPTER TWENTY

What I Have Learned

The last five years have been a roller coaster. There have been a lot of ups and downs but I would not change anything that has happened. I am starting to learn who I am and what I want out of my life. Even though I moved away, my relationship with my family is improving every day and I am very thankful for that. We have all made mistakes, but we all want a good relationship and to be loved.

One evening I was having a short conversation with my parents about my goals for this book. I remember telling them that I believe God put me through psychosis because He knew I would use my experience to help others someday. God never puts us through something He does not believe we can handle, and I fully intend on using my story to aid in the betterment and reform of mental health.

I was always raised to respect my elders, which I do, but as I grow older I have also realized in certain situations that respect needs to be earned and not given. Just because someone is your elder does not give them the right to walk all over you. When I was younger, I never had any boundaries, and I am learning to develop boundaries in order to protect myself and my mental health.

Another important thing I have learned to do is relax. For about twenty-six years I was so high strung that I thrived on stress. I would feel weird if I was not stressed out at some point every day. I have decided that it is okay to be stressed but it is not okay to let it consume you. I have finally mastered ways to bring peace into my life which makes it much more enjoyable.

One main cause of stress in my life was obsessive planning. I would plan my day, plan my future, and if it did not go according to plan, I would ultimately freak out. Now a days I take life more as it comes and I do not stress if something does not go according to plan. I still plan out my life a bit but the emphasis I put on planning is substantially less. I am learning new things about myself every day, and I am proud of the person I am becoming.

I have started to take in more of the beauty of the world; moving to Tennessee has helped with that. I love where I live, so much I took up photography as a hobby just to be able to capture and remember this state's beauty.

The last few months I have also been growing apart from my husband. Although I love him very much, I feel this last year with our struggles and how we dealt with them has caused us to grow apart. I do not feel we are a good match anymore. I told him I wanted a divorce a few weeks ago and we are starting that process, but that is a story for another time.

So here I am now, alone in Tennessee, and living my life to the fullest. I'm focusing on my happiness, finding out who I am, working on my mental health, and hoping I do not pop another tire.

ABOUT THE AUTHOR

Born in New York unto a military family, I've spent the last 28 years navigating this crazy world. Though there were unexpected trials and tribulations, it has been, and continues to be, a good life. I joined the Navy after graduation, which began a whirlwind of consequences that forever changed me.

I received my Bachelor's Degree in Business from San Diego Christian College, as well as a Master's in Project Management from Grantham University. While going to classes at Grantham, I began writing this book to aid in my recovery from mental and physical struggles. But I also wrote it to help others who have fought the same battles.

I found love, comfort, and my path to success thanks to the story told in his book.

Currently residing in Tennessee, I have received a great job offer from The United States Post Office and I am excited to start a new career, as well as continue on my journey of self-discovery.